KIDNEY DISORDERS

GENERAL EDITORS

Dale C. Garell, M.D.
Associate Dean for Curriculum; Clinical Professor, Department of Pediatrics &
    Family Medicine, University of Southern California School of Medicine
Former President, Society for Adolescent Medicine

Solomon H. Snyder, M.D.
Distinguished Service Professor of Neuroscience, Pharmacology, and Psychiatry,
    Johns Hopkins University School of Medicine
Former President, Society for Neuroscience
Albert Lasker Award in Medical Research, 1978

CONSULTING EDITORS

Robert W. Blum, M.D., Ph.D.
Professor and Director, Division of General Pediatrics and Adolescent Health,
    University of Minnesota

Charles E. Irwin, Jr., M.D.
Professor of Pediatrics; Director, Division of Adolescent Medicine, University of
    California, San Francisco

Lloyd J. Kolbe, Ph.D.
Director of the Division of Adolescent and School Health, Center for Chronic
    Disease Prevention and Health Promotion, Centers for Disease Control

Jordan J. Popkin
Former Director, Division of Federal Employee Occupational Health, U.S. Public
    Health Service Region I

Joseph L. Rauh, M.D.
Professor of Pediatrics and Medicine, Adolescent Medicine, Children's Hospital
    Medical Center, Cincinnati
Former President, Society for Adolescent Medicine

Ira Greifer, M.D.
Director of the Children's Kidney Center, Albert Einstein College of Medicine
Medical Director, National Kidney Foundation

THE ENCYCLOPEDIA OF
HEALTH

MEDICAL DISORDERS
AND THEIR TREATMENT

Dale C. Garell, M.D. • General Editor

KIDNEY DISORDERS

Martha J. Miller

Introduction by C. Everett Koop, M.D., Sc.D.

former Surgeon General, U. S. Public Health Service

CHELSEA HOUSE PUBLISHERS

New York • Philadelphia

The goal of the ENCYCLOPEDIA OF HEALTH *is to provide general information in the ever-changing areas of physiology, psychology, and related medical issues. The titles in this series are not intended to take the place of the professional advice of a physician or other health care professional.*

ON THE COVER: Drawing by Leonardo da Vinci

CHELSEA HOUSE PUBLISHERS
EDITOR-IN-CHIEF   Remmel Nunn
MANAGING EDITOR   Karyn Gullen Browne
PICTURE EDITOR   Adrian G. Allen
ART DIRECTOR   Maria Epes
ASSISTANT ART DIRECTOR   Howard Brotman
MANUFACTURING DIRECTOR   Gerald Levine
SYSTEMS MANAGER   Lindsey Ottman
PRODUCTION MANAGER   Joseph Romano
PRODUCTION COORDINATOR   Marie Claire Cebrián

The Encyclopedia of Health
SENIOR EDITOR   Brian Feinberg

Staff for KIDNEY DISORDERS
COPY EDITOR   Laurie Kahn
EDITORIAL ASSISTANT   Tamar Levovitz
PICTURE RESEARCHER   Nisa Rauschenberg
DESIGNER   Robert Yaffe

First Printing
1   3   5   7   9   8   6   4   2

Library of Congress Cataloging-in-Publication Data

Miller, Martha J.
   Kidney disorders/by Martha Miller; introduction by C. Everett Koop.
      p. cm.—(The Encyclopedia of health. Medical disorders and their treatment)
   Includes bibliographical references and index.
   Summary: Discusses how the kidney functions, diseases that can affect it, and ways to treat renal failure.
   ISBN 0-7910-0066-4
         0-7910-0493-7 (pbk.)
   1. Kidneys—Diseases—Juvenile literature. [1. Kidneys—Diseases.] I. Title. II. Series.   91-41299
RC902.M57 1992   CIP
616.6'1—dc20   AC

CONTENTS

THE ENCYCLOPEDIA OF
H E A L T H

THE HEALTHY BODY

The Circulatory System
Dental Health
The Digestive System
The Endocrine System
Exercise
Genetics & Heredity
The Human Body: An Overview
Hygiene
The Immune System
Memory & Learning
The Musculoskeletal System
The Nervous System
Nutrition
The Reproductive System
The Respiratory System
The Senses
Sleep
Speech & Hearing
Sports Medicine
Vision
Vitamins & Minerals

THE LIFE CYCLE

Adolescence
Adulthood
Aging
Childhood
Death & Dying
The Family
Friendship & Love
Pregnancy & Birth

MEDICAL ISSUES

Careers in Health Care
Environmental Health
Folk Medicine
Health Care Delivery
Holistic Medicine
Medical Ethics
Medical Fakes & Frauds
Medical Technology
Medicine & the Law
Occupational Health
Public Health

PSYCHOLOGICAL DISORDERS AND THEIR TREATMENT

Anxiety & Phobias
Child Abuse
Compulsive Behavior
Delinquency & Criminal Behavior
Depression
Diagnosing & Treating Mental Illness
Eating Habits & Disorders
Learning Disabilities
Mental Retardation
Personality Disorders
Schizophrenia
Stress Management
Suicide

MEDICAL DISORDERS AND THEIR TREATMENT

AIDS
Allergies
Alzheimer's Disease
Arthritis
Birth Defects
Cancer
The Common Cold
Diabetes
Emergency Medicine
Gynecological Disorders
Headaches
The Hospital
Kidney Disorders
Medical Diagnosis
The Mind-Body Connection
Mononucleosis and Other Infectious Diseases
Nuclear Medicine
Organ Transplants
Pain
Physical Handicaps
Poisons & Toxins
Prescription & OTC Drugs
Sexually Transmitted Diseases
Skin Disorders
Stroke & Heart Disease
Substance Abuse
Tropical Medicine

PREVENTION AND EDUCATION: THE KEYS TO GOOD HEALTH

C. Everett Koop, M.D., Sc.D.
former Surgeon General,
U.S. Public Health Service

The issue of health education has received particular attention in recent years because of the presence of AIDS in the news. But our response to this particular tragedy points up a number of broader issues that doctors, public health officials, educators, and the public face. In particular, it points up the necessity for sound health education for citizens of all ages.

Over the past 25 years this country has been able to bring about dramatic declines in the death rates for heart disease, stroke, accidents, and for people under the age of 45, cancer. Today, Americans generally eat better and take better care of themselves than ever before. Thus, with the help of modern science and technology, they have a better chance of surviving serious—even catastrophic—illnesses. That's the good news.

But, like every phonograph record, there's a flip side, and one with special significance for young adults. According to a report issued in 1979 by Dr. Julius Richmond, my predecessor as Surgeon General, Americans aged 15 to 24 had a higher death rate in 1979 than they did 20 years earlier. The causes: violent death and injury, alcohol and drug abuse, unwanted pregnancies, and sexually transmitted diseases. Adolescents are particularly vulnerable because they are beginning to explore their own sexuality and perhaps to experiment with drugs. The need for educating young people is critical, and the price of neglect is high.

Yet even for the population as a whole, our health is still far from what it could be. Why? A 1974 Canadian government report attributed all death and disease to four broad elements: inadequacies in the health care system, behavioral factors or unhealthy life-styles, environmental hazards, and human biological factors.

To be sure, there are diseases that are still beyond the control of even our advanced medical knowledge and techniques. And despite yearnings that are as old as the human race itself, there is no "fountain of youth" to ward off aging and death. Still, there is a solution to many of the problems that undermine sound health. In a word, that solution is prevention. Prevention, which includes health promotion and education, saves lives, improves the quality of life, and in the long run, saves money.

In the United States, organized public health activities and preventive medicine have a long history. Important milestones in this country or foreign breakthroughs adopted in the United States include the improvement of sanitary procedures and the development of pasteurized milk in the late 19th century and the introduction in the mid-20th century of effective vaccines against polio, measles, German measles, mumps, and other once-rampant diseases. Internationally, organized public health efforts began on a wide-scale basis with the International Sanitary Conference of 1851, to which 12 nations sent representatives. The World Health Organization, founded in 1948, continues these efforts under the aegis of the United Nations, with particular emphasis on combating communicable diseases and the training of health care workers.

Despite these accomplishments, much remains to be done in the field of prevention. For too long, we have had a medical care system that is science- and technology-based, focused, essentially, on illness and mortality. It is now patently obvious that both the social and the economic costs of such a system are becoming insupportable.

Implementing prevention—and its corollaries, health education and promotion—is the job of several groups of people.

First, the medical and scientific professions need to continue basic scientific research, and here we are making considerable progress. But increased concern with prevention will also have a decided impact on how primary care doctors practice medicine. With a shift to health-based rather than morbidity-based medicine, the role of the "new physician" will include a healthy dose of patient education.

Second, practitioners of the social and behavioral sciences—psychologists, economists, city planners—along with lawyers, business leaders, and government officials—must solve the practical and ethical dilemmas confronting us: poverty, crime, civil rights, literacy, education, employment, housing, sanitation, environmental protection, health care delivery systems, and so forth. All of these issues affect public health.

Third is the public at large. We'll consider that very important group in a moment.

Fourth, and the linchpin in this effort, is the public health profession—doctors, epidemiologists, teachers—who must harness the professional expertise of the first two groups and the common sense and cooperation of the third, the public. They must define the problems statistically and qualitatively and then help us set priorities for finding the solutions.

To a very large extent, improving those statistics is the responsibility of every individual. So let's consider more specifically what the role of the individual should be and why health education is so important to that role. First, and most obvious, individuals can protect themselves from illness and injury and thus minimize their need for professional medical care. They can eat nutritious food; get adequate exercise; avoid tobacco, alcohol, and drugs; and take prudent steps to avoid accidents. The proverbial "apple a day keeps the doctor away" is not so far from the truth, after all.

Second, individuals should actively participate in their own medical care. They should schedule regular medical and dental checkups. Should they develop an illness or injury, they should know when to treat themselves and when to seek professional help. To gain the maximum benefit from any medical treatment that they do require, individuals must become partners in that treatment. For instance, they should understand the effects and side effects of medications. I counsel young physicians that there is no such thing as too much information when talking with patients. But the corollary is the patient must know enough about the nuts and bolts of the healing process to understand what the doctor is telling him or her. That is at least partially the patient's responsibility.

Education is equally necessary for us to understand the ethical and public policy issues in health care today. Sometimes individuals will encounter these issues in making decisions about their own treatment or that of family members. Other citizens may encounter them as jurors in medical malpractice cases. But we all become involved, indirectly, when we elect our public officials, from school board members to the president. Should surrogate parenting be legal? To what extent is drug testing desirable, legal, or necessary? Should there be public funding for family planning, hospitals, various types of medical research, and other medical care for the indigent? How should we allocate scant technological resources, such as kidney dialysis and organ transplants? What is the proper role of government in protecting the rights of patients?

What are the broad goals of public health in the United States today? In 1980, the Public Health Service issued a report aptly entitled *Promoting Health—Preventing Disease: Objectives for the Nation*. This report expressed its goals in terms of mortality and in terms of intermediate goals in education and health improvement. It identified 15 major concerns: controlling high blood pressure; improving family planning; improving pregnancy care and infant health; increasing the rate of immunization; controlling sexually transmitted diseases; controlling the presence of toxic agents and radiation in the environment; improving occupational safety and health; preventing accidents; promoting water fluoridation and dental health; controlling infectious diseases; decreasing smoking; decreasing alcohol and drug abuse; improving nutrition; promoting physical fitness and exercise; and controlling stress and violent behavior.

For healthy adolescents and young adults (ages 15 to 24), the specific goal was a 20% reduction in deaths, with a special focus on motor vehicle injuries and alcohol and drug abuse. For adults (ages 25 to 64), the aim was 25% fewer deaths, with a concentration on heart attacks, strokes, and cancers.

Smoking is perhaps the best example of how individual behavior can have a direct impact on health. Today, cigarette smoking is recognized as the single most important preventable cause of death in our society. It is responsible for more cancers and more cancer deaths than any other known agent; is a prime risk factor for heart and blood vessel disease, chronic bronchitis, and emphysema; and is a frequent cause of complications in pregnancies and of babies born prematurely, underweight, or with potentially fatal respiratory and cardiovascular problems.

Since the release of the Surgeon General's first report on smoking in 1964, the proportion of adult smokers has declined substantially, from 43% in 1965 to 30.5% in 1985. Since 1965, 37 million people have quit smoking. Although there is still much work to be done if we are to become a "smoke-free society," it is heartening to note that public health and public education efforts—such as warnings on cigarette packages and bans on broadcast advertising—have already had significant effects.

In 1835, Alexis de Tocqueville, a French visitor to America, wrote, "In America the passion for physical well-being is general." Today, as then, health and fitness are front-page items. But with the greater scientific and technological resources now available to us, we are in a far stronger position to make good health care available to everyone. And with the greater technological threats to us as we approach the 21st century, the need to do so is more urgent than ever before. Comprehensive information about basic biology, preventive medicine, medical and surgical treatments, and related ethical and public policy issues can help you arm yourself with the knowledge you need to be healthy throughout your life.

FOREWORD

Dale C. Garell, M.D.

Advances in our understanding of health and disease during the 20th century have been truly remarkable. Indeed, it could be argued that modern health care is one of the greatest accomplishments in all of human history. In the early 20th century, improvements in sanitation, water treatment, and sewage disposal reduced death rates and increased longevity. Previously untreatable illnesses can now be managed with antibiotics, immunizations, and modern surgical techniques. Discoveries in the fields of immunology, genetic diagnosis, and organ transplantation are revolutionizing the prevention and treatment of disease. Modern medicine is even making inroads against cancer and heart disease, two of the leading causes of death in the United States.

Although there is much to be proud of, medicine continues to face enormous challenges. Science has vanquished diseases such as smallpox and polio, but new killers, most notably AIDS, confront us. Moreover, we now victimize ourselves with what some have called "diseases of choice," or those brought on by drug and alcohol abuse, bad eating habits, and mismanagement of the stresses and strains of contemporary life. The very technology that is doing so much to prolong life has brought with it previously unimaginable ethical dilemmas related to issues of death and dying. The rising cost of health care is a matter of central concern to us all. And violence in the form of automobile accidents, homicide, and suicide remains the major killer of young adults.

In the past, most people were content to leave health care and medical treatment in the hands of professionals. But since the 1960s, the consumer of medical care—that is, the patient—has assumed an increasingly central role in the management of his or her own health. There has also been a new emphasis placed on prevention: People are recognizing that their own actions can help prevent many of the conditions that have caused death and disease in the past. This accounts for the growing commitment to good nutrition and regular exercise, for the increasing number of people who are choosing not to smoke, and for a new moderation in people's drinking habits.

People want to know more about themselves and their own health. They are curious about their body: its anatomy, physiology, and biochemistry. They want to keep up with rapidly evolving medical technologies and procedures. They are willing to educate themselves about common disorders and diseases so that they can be full partners in their own health care.

THE ENCYCLOPEDIA OF HEALTH is designed to provide the basic knowledge that readers will need if they are to take significant responsibility for their own health. It is also meant to serve as a frame of reference for further study and exploration. The encyclopedia is divided into five subsections: The Healthy Body; The Life Cycle; Medical Disorders & Their Treatment; Psychological Disorders & Their Treatment; and Medical Issues. For each topic covered by the encyclopedia, we present the essential facts about the relevant biology; the symptoms, diagnosis, and treatment of common diseases and disorders; and ways in which you can prevent or reduce the severity of health problems when that is possible. The encyclopedia also projects what may lie ahead in the way of future treatment or prevention strategies.

The broad range of topics and issues covered in the encyclopedia reflects that human health encompasses physical, psychological, social, environmental, and spiritual well-being. Just as the mind and the body are inextricably linked, so, too, is the individual an integral part of the wider world that comprises his or her family, society, and environment. To discuss health in its broadest aspect it is necessary to explore the many ways in which it is connected to such fields as law, social science, public policy, economics, and even religion. And so, the encyclopedia is meant to be a bridge between science, medical technology, the world at large, and you. I hope that it will inspire you to pursue in greater depth particular areas of interest and that you will take advantage of the suggestions for further reading and the lists of resources and organizations that can provide additional information.

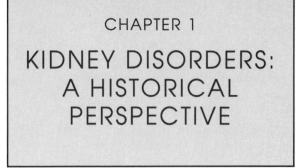

CHAPTER 1

KIDNEY DISORDERS: A HISTORICAL PERSPECTIVE

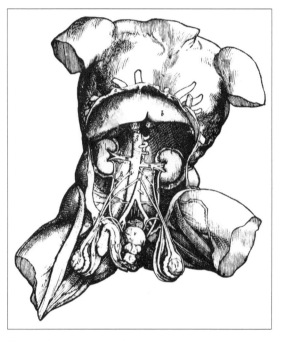

The kidneys, bean-shaped organs in the middle of the torso, maintain a proper balance of materials in the bloodstream and remove harmful wastes from the body.

An estimated 20 million Americans suffer from diseases of the kidney or urinary tract, according to the National Kidney Foundation. But as a result of the advent of new technology, medicines, and medical techniques, doctors can now routinely save kidney patients who only 30 years ago would have had little, if any, chance of survival. The medical field's growing understanding of kidney disorders and the life-saving advances that have resulted, are among the focuses of this book. As an introduction to these topics, a short discussion of the organ and its function is in order.

BASIC STRUCTURE AND FUNCTION OF THE KIDNEYS

The 2 kidneys, each about 4 1/2 inches long, are located on either side of the spine, toward the back of the torso. Weighing between 4 1/2 and 5 ounces, they are situated in the middle of the body, approximately level with the small of the back, where they have access to major blood vessels.

The right kidney is slightly lower than the left because it is displaced downward by the mass of the liver; both are well protected by the muscles of the abdomen and back and by a surrounding capsule of fat.

The kidneys maintain a proper balance of a variety of substances in the bloodstream and remove waste products from the body so that they do not reach harmful levels. Unneeded substances are eliminated in the form of *urine*, a combination of excess water and waste.

Despite the fact that humans are born with two kidneys, it is possible to live a normal life with just one. Therefore, a healthy person can donate a kidney to a patient whose own kidneys are not functioning. The donor's single remaining kidney will enlarge and take on the work load of the missing organ.

In some places throughout this text, the word *renal* may appear in place of the word *kidney*. The terms can be used interchangeably—for example, kidney disease is also called renal disease—because *renal* means "pertaining to the kidneys."

KIDNEY DISORDERS IN HISTORY

Although there have been recent advances in the diagnosis and treatment of kidney disease, very little was understood about the kidney until the late 19th century. Only 100 years ago, one physician complained, "All we know for certain about the kidney is that it makes

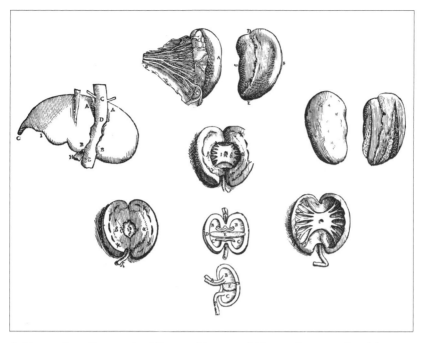

Art based on the work of the well-known 16th-century anatomist Andreas Vesalius (1514–64). Despite early strides in understanding kidney structure and disease, much about the organ remained shrouded in mystery even a century ago.

urine." Because of this lack of knowledge, kidney diseases, although frequently noted, were typically misunderstood and inadequately treated.

The Greek physician Hippocrates (ca. 460– ca. 377 B.C.), the Father of Medicine, provided insight into the workings of the organ by recognizing the existence of kidney disorders. He even linked some of his diagnoses to abnormalities in the urine. Blood or pus in the urine was an indication of infection; bubbles on the surface were associated with kidney failure; sudden appearance of blood was linked to hemorrhage; and sandy sediment indicated the possible existence of *kidney stones* (hard particles formed from substances that precipitate out of the urine). Although Hippocrates cautioned physicians against surgically removing these stones, he did recommend treatment with bleedings and with potions containing such ingredients as ox dung and copper.

In time, other views of kidney function were advanced. In the 2nd century A.D., for example, the Greek physician Galen (129–ca. 199) thought that there were sieves inside the kidney that helped filter out impurities and waste products from the bloodstream into the urine. This idea, which essentially was not far from the truth, persisted for many centuries.

Urine Analysis

Like Hippocrates, later physicians also used urine as a means of diagnosing illness. In 9th-century Salerno, Italy, doctors were studying the work of Isaac Judaeus, a medieval master who scrupulously analyzed many facets of urine, including color, odor, and sediment.

For a time, physicians used urine analysis (also referred to as *urinalysis*) to the exclusion of other techniques, even though the

Since premodern times, physicians have understood the importance of diagnosing disease through urine analysis, although for a time the practice was overused.

resulting diagnoses were often dangerously inaccurate. By the 16th century, the problem apparently had become so great that the Royal College of Physicians in London denounced treatments based solely upon the examination of urine.

As the pendulum swung back toward moderation, though, doctors became more measured in their use of urinalysis as a diagnostic tool. It was not abandoned, however, and the work of Dutch researcher Frederick Deckers (1648–1720) reminded scientists that this technique could still be quite useful. Deckers found that if he heated certain urine samples they would coagulate. Ultimately, this clotting was associated with the presence of protein in the urine and became a very significant reflection of diseases, such as *nephritis* (inflammation of the kidney) or *nephrosis* (a disorder characterized by the retention of fluid in the body). In the early 19th century, British physician Richard Bright said,

Italian anatomist Marcello Malpighi's discovery of small, ball-like structures in the kidney challenged then-accepted theories of kidney anatomy.

"I have never yet examined the body of a patient dying with dropsy attended with coagulable urine, in whom some obvious derangement was not discovered in the kidneys."

Before the 18th century, much emphasis had been placed upon substances that appeared abnormally in the urine. Blood, pus, sediment, protein, and sugar were all studied and associated in some way with disease. By the 1770s, new work was being done that enabled scientists to identify *urea*, a waste product produced when the body uses protein. Urea is the primary waste normally eliminated by the kidneys. When kidney function fails, urea cannot be eliminated sufficiently, and when it accumulates in the bloodstream, a life-threatening condition called *uremia* develops. (This will be more fully discussed in Chapter 6.)

Advanced View of Anatomy and Function

With the advent of the microscope, major steps could be made toward developing a more realistic kidney model. In 1659, for example, the Italian anatomist Marcello Malpighi (1628–94) discovered the existence of "little balls" within the kidney. By challenging, at least in part, Galen's "sieve" theory, he incurred the wrath of outraged colleagues who resisted change and stood loyally behind an outdated concept.

Fortunately, his findings were not totally discarded, and in 1842, Sir William Bowman (1816–92), a British physician, reexamined Malpighi's work and found it to be basically sound. Bowman, however, went one step further and identified one of the central mechanisms involved in urine formation—the process of *filtration*.

He discovered that the many "balls" inside the kidney were, in fact, cuplike structures that were a part of every *nephron* (the small structural unit in the kidney that acts as a filter for urine). One of these cups, now called a *Bowman's capsule*, is located at the beginning of each nephron. Each capsule contains a small sphere of capillaries called a *glomerulus*. (Capillaries are minute blood vessels connecting the body's artery system to the system of veins.) Urine formation is started when fluid passes through the wall of the capillaries and filters into the cuplike receptacle of the nephron.

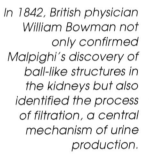

In 1842, British physician William Bowman not only confirmed Malpighi's discovery of ball-like structures in the kidneys but also identified the process of filtration, a central mechanism of urine production.

It was not until 1917, during World War I, that a Scottish professor of pharmacology, A. R. Cushny, elaborated upon the *reabsorption* mechanism associated with urine production. Through this mechanism, substances that have filtered into the nephron—but are still needed by the body—are absorbed back into the bloodstream instead of being eliminated.

Early Treatment of Kidney Stones   *Important*

Typically, urine formed in the kidney flows through narrow tubes called *ureters* into the *urinary bladder*, a muscular container. When the bladder becomes full, pressure is exerted that triggers the voluntary release of urine from the bladder through another tube, the *urethra*.

Sometimes the flow of urine is impeded by structures that block the tubes. This blockage can result in the retention of urine, that is, an inability to urinate or empty the bladder. In the worst cases, urine will actually back up or reverse direction and return to the kidneys, often resulting in renal infection. *Chronic*, or long-lasting, infection will ultimately interfere with kidney function.

One cause of obstruction that has received much attention historically is the formation of kidney stones, also known as *calculi*. Hippocrates cautioned physicians against practicing *lithotomy* (cutting for stones), and for many centuries, the messy business of such renal surgery was left to "specialists," many of whom were not qualified to

An early operation to remove kidney stones (lithotomy); before the advent of anesthesia, sterile technique, and properly trained physicians, such surgery often proved fatal.

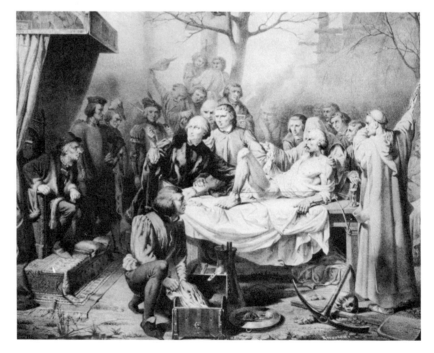

practice surgery. Without anesthesia, sterile technique, or a skilled surgeon, such operations often proved fatal in centuries past.

Some people, in fact, chose pain and suffering rather than the knife. One case in point was Benjamin Franklin (1706–90), who was plagued throughout his life with kidney stones. He had excruciating pain, blood in his urine, and interrupted urine flow, but he still refused to undergo surgery. He spent his last years in bed, reduced to a skeleton—and his situation was not unique.

Many, on the other hand, risked death to bring an end to the symptoms associated with calculi. Among them were the English diarist Samuel Pepys (1633–1703) and U.S. Supreme Court chief justice John Marshall (1755–1835).

By the 16th century, Ambroise Paré (1510–90), a French barber and surgeon, had written extensively on the technique of *perineal lithotomy*. This common type of surgery involved making an incision in the groin. The master of perineal lithotomies was Pierre Franco, who also practiced in 16th-century France. He was also the first to describe the *supra-pubic lithotomy* (performed through an incision made in the lower abdomen), the technique that is most commonly used today. It was Franco who challenged historical procedure and recommended a two-stage lithotomy. He suggested making the incision first, and then, a few days later, removing the stone. He also believed in leaving the wound open to heal, a technique that was found to be very successful.

For centuries, however, lithotomy remained a relatively crude procedure by modern standards. This changed somewhat in the 18th century, with the advent of professional lithotomists. William Cheselden (1688–1752), of St. Thomas's Hospital in London, was able to reduce the time needed to remove a stone from more than an hour to less than a minute. The public became so fascinated by the work of lithotomists that watching the surgery actually became a type of spectator's activity.

In 1881, the work of British surgeon Joseph Lister (1827–1912) brought sterile technique into the operating room. By reducing the risk of infection, he made it possible to perform supra-pubic lithotomies more frequently and with greater success.

William Cheselden, an 18th-century British surgeon, reduced the time needed to remove a kidney stone from more than an hour to less than a minute.

Currently, surgery is only one treatment option for patients suffering from kidney stones. It is often possible to avoid surgery by using the process of shock disintegration—known as *extracorporeal shock wave lithotripsy*—to crush the stones. This technique was greeted with much fanfare in renal medicine circles. It provides the opportunity to treat kidney stones with minimal tissue trauma and relatively little patient inconvenience or pain. The method will be discussed further in Chapter 5.

Early Prostate Treatment

Though not itself a kidney disorder, urine retention—and, potentially, kidney infection—in men can also result from an enlarged *prostate gland*. This gland, found only in males, is shaped like a doughnut and surrounds the urethra at the base of the bladder. It produces a milky fluid used in the production of semen. Infection, cancer, or old age can

In 1881, the work of British surgeon Joseph Lister brought sterile technique to the operating room, making surgery—including the removal of kidney stones—safer.

cause the prostate to enlarge, and when it does, the gland can place pressure on the urethra, preventing the free flow of urine.

Before the advent of surgical relief, the only viable treatment option when the prostate blocked the urinary tract was the *catheter*, a narrow tube carefully inserted up through the urethra into the bladder. Utilized as far back as the days of ancient Rome, it came into more frequent use toward the end of the Middle Ages.

Catheters came in many materials. Gold and silver were prevalent during the Middle Ages, and by the end of the 17th century, gold alone was favored. Throughout most of the 19th century, catheterization became the treatment of choice for older men with prostate trouble. Many wealthy patients would buy a seven-day set of catheters. These were often hidden in the hollowed out handles of walking sticks or umbrellas so as to be readily accessible. But the long-term use of catheters carried with it a serious risk of infection.

For this reason, the advent of prostate surgery in the 1830s was a welcome advance. In time, the ability to remove the prostate gland became a reality in both Europe and America. Today, prostate surgery is performed with the help of the *endoscope*, a device consisting of a tube and an optical system for observing the inside of an organ or a cavity.

Gout

Gout is a kidney-related disorder characterized by an excessive amount of *uric acid* in the bloodstream. This imbalance may be caused either by overproduction of uric acid or by impaired kidney function that prevents the organ from properly eliminating uric acid from the body. As a result, *urate crystals* are deposited in joint cavities and within the urinary tract.

Symptoms of gout can range from excruciating pain upon movement of the affected joints to kidney failure brought on by interference

Old-fashioned kidney medication

YOU WILL NEVER REGRET TRYING

The Great Sierra Kidney and Liver Cure

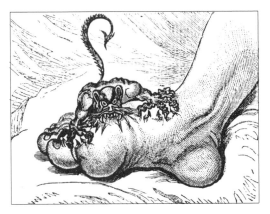

Artist's impression of gout pain (1799); the disorder, which occurs when the kidneys cannot properly eliminate uric acid, causes painful urate crystals to collect in joint cavities and in the urinary tract.

with renal function. Even 20 years ago, gout-related kidney damage caused 10,000 deaths per year in the United States alone according to the book *The Kidneys: Balancing the Fluids* (Torstar Books, 1985).

Hippocrates referred to gout as *podagra*. In his day, it was believed to be a disease of excess—too much wine, food, and sex. Centuries later, one gout victim, British physician Thomas Sydenham (1624–89), wrote an important treatise on the disease in which he distinguished it from other joint disorders. British essayist Sydney Smith (1771–1845) claimed that the pain of gout was "like walking on my eyeballs, or like having my ankle crushed in a flaming vise."

Historic victims of gout include a long list of the powerful and famous: Kublai Khan, Alexander the Great, Charlemagne, Lord (George Gordon) Byron, John Milton, Robert Browning, Lewis Carroll, Alfred Tennyson, Johann Wolfgang von Goethe, Charles Darwin, Isaac Newton, and Bernard Baruch. Below are just three examples of historical literary references made to gout.

> Just as old age is creeping on apace
> And clouds come o'er the sunset of our day,
> They kindly leave us, though not quite alone
> In good company with the gout or stone.
> —Lord Byron

> A taste for drink, combined with gout,
> Had doubled him up forever.

Of that there is no manner of doubt—
No probable, possible shadow of doubt—
No possible doubt whatever.
—From a Gilbert and Sullivan operetta

Lazy Tom with jacket blue
Stole his father's gouty shoe.
The worst of harm that Dad can wish him
Is that his gouty shoe might fit him.
—From a Mother Goose rhyme

An estimated 1 million Americans suffer from gout, according to the Arthritis Foundation. Although the disease appears to be hereditary, 80% of its victims are male. Today the threat of gout is minimized by medications that can control the symptoms or the uric acid imbalance itself. Drugs commonly used include the anti-inflammatory agents colchicine or phenylbutazone; allopurinol, which decreases the formation of uric acid; and probenecid or sulfinpyrazone, both of which increase the excretion of uric acid.

In 1913, dialysis on animals was first attempted by John Abel of the Johns Hopkins University.

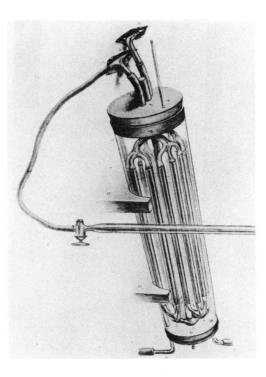

A dialysis machine from about 1913

Dialysis

Not many years ago, when the kidneys became diseased or injured and unable to function properly, the prospect for survival was bleak. Kidney failure would allow toxins, or poisons, to accumulate in the bloodstream, ultimately resulting in the victim's death.

As early as the mid-19th century, a Scottish chemist named Thomas Graham (1805–69) envisioned a way to sidestep the problems of renal failure with a process called *dialysis*. In this procedure, blood from the patient would be separated from a balanced fluid by a *selectively permeable membrane* (a membrane that allows only certain types of molecules to pass through). Toxins would pass out of the bloodstream, through the membrane, and into the dialysate fluid, while needed minerals and other chemicals could replenish the *plasma* (the liquid portion of blood).

It was not until 1913 that dialysis was first attempted on animals by John Abel at the Johns Hopkins University. But the tendency of

blood to clot when it passed through the tubes of the machine remained a big obstacle to successful dialysis treatment.

By the end of World War II, however, many advances had been
made, and the crude prototype of a *kidney machine* had been developed. Today dialysis is a common, but essential, part of treatment for
kidney disorders. The procedure will be examined in greater detail in
Chapter 7.

Kidney Transplants

Once considered to be within the realm of science fiction, kidney
transplants are now fairly routine. In 1990, about 9,800 kidney trans-

*French surgeon Alexis
Carrel invented the tiny
needles and sutures re-
quired for transplant
surgery.*

plants were performed in the United States, according to the U.S. Health Care Financing Administration. Although successful transplants are a phenomenon of the 20th century, their historical origins run far back in time. As early as 300 B.C., for example, skin grafts were performed in India. During the 16th century, as a result of traders' contact with the West, such surgical techniques were carried to Europe.

Many factors made surgery difficult, however. There were no *anesthetics* (medicines to kill pain) and no *antibiotics* (drugs to fight infection). Additionally, the Catholic church spoke out against grafting, accusing physicians of interfering with the will of God. As time passed, however, the world became more open to the concept of such surgery, and by the 18th century, British surgeons were once again using this technique.

In 1901, Viennese scientist Karl Landsteiner discovered that blood could be classified by the type of protein found in the membrane of the blood cells. This breakthrough was an early step toward discovering the concepts of tissue compatibility essential to successful organ transplants.

The advent of general anesthesia in the 19th century paralleled reports of transplants of bone, muscle, and limbs. Techniques were also being developed to facilitate the delicate surgical procedures involved in transplants. Because grafting requires the attachment of the transplant recipient's blood vessels to those in the donor tissue, special instruments were needed. It was French surgeon Alexis Carrel (1873–1944) who invented the tiny needles and *sutures*, or threads, so essential to the transplant. The grafts, however, survived for a very limited period—usually no more than a few weeks.

The major reason for rejection of a graft is the body's *immune response*. Within each person, there are substances in the bloodstream designed to fight off foreign "invaders." Bacteria or viruses that enter the system, for example, are attacked by immune cells. If the invasion is limited to a certain area, such as the skin, the immune attack results in redness, heat, and swelling at the affected site. Similarly, when a graft is attempted, the recipient's body treats the new tissue as foreign and mobilizes a campaign to destroy it. The ultimate result of such an attack is rejection of the transplant.

Because it was such an obstacle to a successful graft, much study and time were devoted to finding a way around the immune response. In 1901, initial steps were taken when Viennese scientist Karl Landsteiner (1868–1943) found that blood could be classified by the type of protein found in the membrane of the blood cells. Moreover, it was discovered that if a person received a transfusion from an incompatible donor, types of proteins called *antibodies* in the recipient's blood would attack the incoming cells.

In the early 1950s, doctors first assumed that grafts between people of compatible blood types would prove to be successful. But such was not the case. Testing this premise in 1953 with the first human-to-human kidney transplant resulted in the patient's death almost six months after surgery. Subsequent operations met the same end. Ultimately, it became clear that a compatible blood type could not ensure a successful transplant.

In 1954, however, it was discovered that kidney transplants between identical twins did not meet with rejection problems. By 1960,

30 operations of this type had been completed successfully. Also by that time, the concept of *tissue typing* had been introduced by the British anatomist Peter Medawar. A major breakthrough in the field of immunology, this new technique made it possible to find body cells that would be compatible between a transplant recipient and his or her donor, decreasing the chances of rejection. Identical twins, of course, have identical tissue types. The next best chance for a match is found among the patient's blood relatives—primarily his or her parents or siblings.

But despite these advances, problems with rejection remained. In 1959, Boston physicians Robert Schwartz and William Dameshek discovered that certain medications, known as *immunosuppressive drugs*, could be used to dampen the immune response, and in the 1960s,

By 1960, British anatomist Peter Medawar had introduced the concept of tissue typing, a major breakthrough in the field of immunology and transplant surgery.

treatment with X rays and cortisone drugs were used for this purpose. Unfortunately, this procedure also resulted in decreased protection against infection. Patients therefore had to risk potentially lethal side effects, such as pneumonia and other devastating infectious diseases, in order to decrease the probability of transplant rejection. But adjustments in dosage helped make side effects more tolerable.

In 1972, with the discovery of the immunosuppressive abilities of the drug *cyclosporine*, another large step was taken in the battle against transplant rejections. More effective than any of its predecessors, this medication also lacked the life-threatening side effects posed by other such drugs.

Today improvements in transplant procedures have dramatically increased the number of such operations and their successful completion. As research continues, better drugs and techniques, and decreased complications should maximize the chances for transplant success.

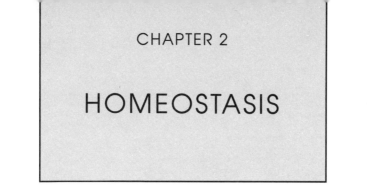

CHAPTER 2

HOMEOSTASIS

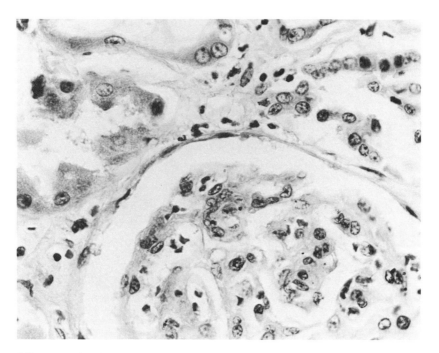

Microscopic photo of a normal kidney cell

Beneath the surface of the healthy human body lie 100 trillion microscopic building blocks called *cells*. These require oxygen and nutrients to stay alive and must have a means of getting rid of the wastes resulting from *metabolic activity*. (*Metabolism* refers to the chemical reactions that occur within the cell.) Furthermore, if the cells are to survive, *intracellular fluid* (the fluid within the cells) and *interstitial fluid* (the fluid that surrounds and bathes the outside of the cells) must be regulated so that content varies very little. The maintenance of a constant environment is known as *homeostasis*. By eliminating waste products in the form of urine, the kidneys play a very important role in homeostasis.

BODY FLUIDS, NUTRIENTS, AND WASTE PRODUCTS

Although not immediately evident to the naked eye, fluid accounts for a large percentage of body weight. In the average adult male, 60% of body weight is fluid. Over the course of a lifetime, the fluid share of body weight decreases from about 80% at infancy to between 40% and 50% in old age. This fluid, moreover, is distributed among three areas. The body contains about 25 liters of intracellular fluid, 12 liters of interstitial fluid, and approximately 3 liters of plasma. (Interstitial fluid and plasma together are referred to as *extracellular fluid*.) All together, the body contains about 40 liters, or more than 40 quarts, of fluid.

Mixed with the water contained in body fluids are substances called *electrolytes*, so named because they take on an electric charge when mixed into a solution. Among the prevalent electrolytes in body fluids are sodium, potassium, calcium, chloride, and bicarbonate. Protein particles are also found in fluid inside and outside the cells.

To sustain health, it is important not only to maintain an adequate volume of water, electrolytes, and proteins in the body fluids but also to preserve their balance and distribution. Intracellular fluid is separated from the interstitial fluid by a thin membrane surrounding each cell. Plasma, in turn, is separated from the interstitial fluid by the walls of the blood vessels. Electrolytes are also selectively distributed. Sodium and chloride, for example, are found primarily in the interstitial fluid, whereas potassium and calcium tend to be concentrated within the cell itself.

It is also essential to prevent wastes from building up in cells. When food is eaten, the nutrients are broken down chemically in the stomach and intestines into particles small enough to pass from the gastrointestinal tract into the bloodstream. Carbohydrates are broken down into *glucose*. (Glucose is a *simple sugar* used to make more complex sugars and starches.) Proteins are broken down into *amino acids*, and fats into

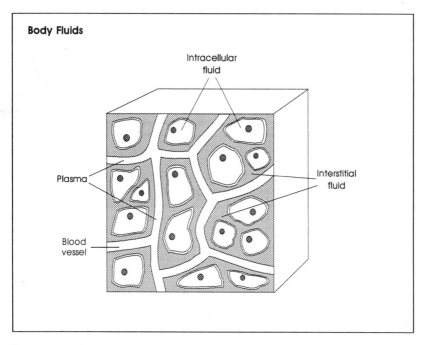

Body Fluids

Intracellular fluid

Plasma

Blood vessel

Interstitial fluid

The human body contains more than 40 quarts of fluid—which comprises intracellular fluid, interstitial fluid, and plasma.

fatty acids and *glycerol*. These products can then either be stored in the body or carried to the cells and burned to generate energy. When glucose, the primary cellular food, is used for energy, it is broken down inside the cells, and carbon dioxide and water are released as waste products. When fatty acids are used to generate energy, substances called *ketone bodies* are released. As mentioned earlier, when amino acids are metabolized, urea is one of the resulting wastes. If allowed to accumulate, these waste products are toxic. Whereas the lungs are responsible for eliminating the majority of excess carbon dioxide, the kidneys play the major role in excreting ketone bodies, urea, and excess water, glucose, and electrolytes.

The kidneys do not function exclusively for waste removal. They also preserve the very delicate balance of electrolytes and help ensure that the body contains enough, but not too much, water. As two of the primary mediators of homeostasis, they are essential to the maintenance of cellular health and thus to the survival of the body as a whole. In the following sections, the importance of fluid and electrolyte balance will be discussed, as well as the kidneys' role in maintaining these balances.

KIDNEYS AND WATER BALANCE

It is common knowledge that water is essential for survival. Without water, cell function would stop and cells would die. Water is also needed to make up the liquid portion of blood. Without plasma, nutrients and oxygen would not be transported to individual cells, and toxic wastes could not be eliminated.

Diagram of the digestive system. When sugars, fats, or proteins are digested, urination is one way that the body eliminates harmful waste products.

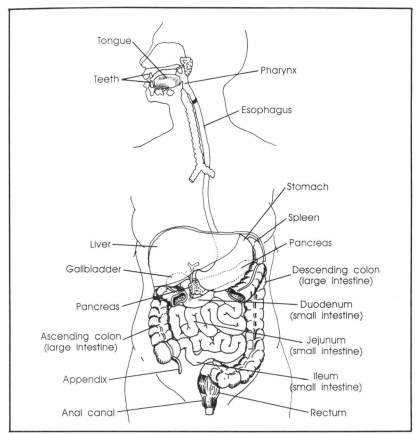

Normally, adults consume about 2,700 milliliters, or about 2 3/4 quarts, of water per day. Although liquids account for a large percentage of intake, solid foods can also have a high water content. Meats and vegetables, for example, may consist of 60% to 95% water. In fact, many animals living in the desert, where water is scarce, can survive primarily on the liquid provided by solid food. Another source of fluid in the body is the water generated when glucose is broken down within cells to release energy. The average metabolism yields about 250 milliliters of water every 24 hours.

To prevent excess fluid from accumulating, the body eliminates water in a variety of ways. Water vapor is excreted along with carbon dioxide every time the lungs exhale. Water is a primary component of perspiration, and feces normally carry enough water to keep stools soft. But, of the 2,500 milliliters of fluid normally eliminated per day, 1,000 to 1,500 or more milliliters are typically excreted by the kidneys in the form of urine. Under normal conditions, intake of fluid should approximately equal output. There are times, however, when imbalances develop.

Water Retention

Female hormones are one factor that can cause the body to retain fluid. For the week to 10 days preceding the onset of menstruation, many women suffer extreme discomfort. Rings and shoes are tight, clothes are snug, feet, ankles, and hands may be puffy, and there is usually a weight gain.

Because the sodium contained in salt "attracts" water (a phenomenon discussed later in this chapter), a high-salt diet can also cause a fluid imbalance. Many prepared foods on the market today contain large amounts of salt—especially prepackaged, canned, preserved, and smoked products. Culprits include many snack foods (such as nuts, chips, and dips), hot dogs, luncheon meat, soda, salad dressing, and frozen TV dinners.

Too much salt in the bloodstream can pose a serious problem to people with high blood pressure or heart disease. By drawing extra water into the blood vessels, high sodium levels can tax an already-strained heart and critically increase the volume of fluid pushing against the blood vessel walls. Because of this potential for cardiovascular overload, it is often recommended that even young, healthy people make a concerted attempt to decrease salt intake.

In the case of kidney failure, however, the problem of fluid retention becomes particularly extreme. If the kidneys are unable to eliminate sufficient water, fluid accumulates in the extracellular areas. In addition to the symptoms of fluid overload already mentioned, *pulmonary edema* (accumulation of fluid in the lungs) can develop over time and, as a result of cardiovascular overload, the neck veins may become swollen and prominent.

Dehydration

At the other extreme of fluid imbalance is *dehydration*, in which the body has insufficient fluid. An athlete exercising strenuously on a hot summer day may develop dehydration because of excessive fluid loss through perspiration. As a result of severe vomiting, diarrhea, or a combination of the two, people suffering from intestinal flu can be in danger of an imbalance.

Exercise, particularly in hot weather, can cause excessive fluid loss. In an attempt to compensate for dehydration, the kidneys decrease the amount of urine they produce.

Regardless of cause, dehydration is usually accompanied by weight loss, sunken eyeballs, and increased body temperature (water is essential to temperature regulation). Dehydration can also lead to low blood volume that, in turn, can cause low blood pressure, resulting in *shock*. (Shock refers to a condition in which bodily functions slow down or stop as a result of a severe injury or other stress to the body that reduces blood flow to vital organs.)

The kidneys, however, can help alleviate the problem. When blood pressure drops too low, the kidneys release the enzyme *renin* into the bloodstream. This chemical promotes the production of the substance *angiotensin I*, which is then transformed by other enzymes into *angiotensin II*, a substance that helps raise blood pressure in two ways: by causing certain small arteries to constrict in size and by stimulating the release of *aldosterone* from the *adrenal glands*. Aldosterone plays a large role in regulating blood pressure, and will be discussed in greater detail in the next section.

ELECTROLYTE BALANCE

Sodium

Sodium is one of the major extracellular electrolytes. It is essential to the normal functioning of both nerve cells and muscle cells and plays an important role in affecting water balance in the body.

Normally, the concentration of sodium in the extracellular fluid is about 3.2 milligrams of sodium for every quart of fluid. Imbalances occur when there are changes in the concentration of sodium in the body. If the sodium concentration is too high, the body can retain too much water in the interstitial fluid and, as mentioned, in the bloodstream as well.

How does excess sodium lead to water retention? This phenomenon is attributed to the process of *osmosis*. During osmosis, water molecules diffuse through a selectively permeable membrane from an area where water molecules are more concentrated to one where they are less concentrated. Water molecules are less concentrated, of course, when other particles, such as sodium atoms, are mixed in among them.

Therefore, when the concentration of sodium in water on side A of a selectively permeable membrane is higher than on side B, the concentration of water molecules on side A is lower than on side B. As a result, more water molecules will travel across the membrane from side B to side A—rather than vice versa—until a balance is reached.

In the body, when extracellular fluid becomes "saltier" than the fluid inside the cells—that is, when the sodium concentration rises—water from the cells crosses the cell membrane into the extracellular areas. The salty extracellular fluid draws an unusually high amount of water out of the gastrointestinal tract, rather than allowing the water to be eliminated from the body. In addition to the effects of water retention previously discussed, this problem can also cause cells to shrink as they lose water to the extracellular areas. Nerve cells are particularly sensitive to water loss, and the result can be restlessness, apprehension, seizures, and in extreme cases, coma.

When the body's sodium concentration falls below normal, the result can be equally serious. In a case of intestinal flu, the body loses both sodium and water through diarrhea and vomiting. Well-meaning friends or relatives often attempt to ward off the sufferer's dehydration by offering water as a replacement for fluid loss. But, if both sodium and water are being eliminated, and only water is being replaced, the sodium left in plasma and interstitial fluid will become increasingly dilute.

Similarly, heavy exercise on an excessively hot day can cause a massive loss of fluid through perspiration. Because sweat contains both sodium and water, drinking pure water to replace the fluid loss will dilute existing sodium levels. For this reason, athletes are usually advised to consume sports drinks containing electrolytes mixed with water during a workout.

When the extracellular concentration of sodium falls, the body is less able to draw water from the cells, which, in turn, begin to swell. This can lead to general weakness, abdominal cramps, nausea, vomiting, and diarrhea. If swelling occurs in the cells of the brain, twitching, disorientation, convulsions, or coma can result.

When a sodium imbalance occurs, regardless of the cause, the kidneys typically work to restore homeostasis. Thus, if the body has

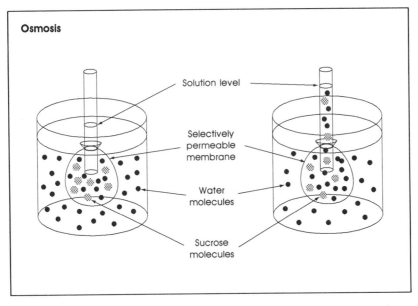

Osmosis

Solution level

Selectively permeable membrane

Water molecules

Sucrose molecules

Osmosis in action. In the diagram on the left, the concentration of water molecules inside the bag is less than the concentration outside because sucrose molecules are taking up space inside the bag, crowding out water molecules. In the diagram on the right, osmosis has occurred, with water molecules moving through the semipermeable membrane into the bag in order to balance the concentration.

too much sodium and too little water, sodium is eliminated and water is retained. Conversely, if the problem is too little sodium or too much water, the kidneys act to retain sodium and eliminate some of the excess water. Aldosterone is essential to this process.

As previously mentioned, when the body's fluid level drops too low, renin is released by the kidneys. This ultimately leads to the secretion of aldosterone from specialized cells located in the outermost layer of the adrenal glands. Located on top of the kidneys, the glands significantly affect metabolism, immunity to disease, and fluid and electrolyte balance. It is under the influence of aldosterone that sodium is reabsorbed from the nephrons back into the bloodstream. Because sodium attracts water, fluid also leaves the nephron.

If, on the other hand, the adrenal glands secrete less than the usual amount of aldosterone or if the action of aldosterone is somehow blocked, then an increased amount of sodium will be eliminated in the urine, taking much of the extracellular water with it and alleviating water retention. Some *diuretics* (substances that increase the elimination of urine) work by making aldosterone less effective.

Potassium

Potassium is another electrolyte found in plasma and interstitial fluid. It is essential to the normal functioning of muscles and nerves in the body. Excess potassium concentration can develop in a number of ways. Most commonly, potassium accumulates when it is not properly eliminated, as in cases of renal failure. It can also increase when there is severe damage to the body cells, caused, for example, by burns, crushing injuries, or lack of oxygen. If the cell membranes are injured, excess potassium leaks from the cells into the plasma and interstitial fluid and causes an increase in extracellular potassium concentration.

Symptoms often associated with excessive potassium include weak muscle contractions, intestinal pain, diarrhea, and *cardiac arrhythmia* (an irregular heartbeat). At the extreme, cardiac arrest will result.

Lack of sufficient potassium can also be life threatening. This imbalance is often caused by excessive urination, vomiting, or diarrhea. Deficiencies develop because fluid flushed out of the body by the intestinal tract or the kidneys often washes a great deal of potassium out with it, largely because the contents of the digestive tract are typically high in potassium.

Currently, much is being written about the eating disorders anorexia nervosa and bulimia. Each year, many young people are affected by these disorders, which can result in an induced potassium imbalance. Anorectics, who routinely starve themselves into a skeletal state, often digest large quantities of laxatives to purge their system of food, causing severe diarrhea. Bulimics, on the other hand, eat large amounts of food and subsequently induce vomiting. In both cases, potassium is swept out of the body as digestive wastes are eliminated in excessive amounts.

Regardless of the cause, an insufficient potassium concentration interferes with both muscle and nerve function. Symptoms include weak, flabby skeletal muscles, bloating, vomiting, and paralysis of the digestive tract. Low blood pressure and arrhythmia can also result.

Whether potassium levels are too low or too high, the kidneys again play a major role in restoring homeostasis, either by retaining or by eliminating the electrolyte. As with sodium, aldosterone is involved in regulating potassium concentration. In this case, the hormone stimulates secretion of potassium into the nephrons. When potassium levels in the blood are high, the aldosterone concentration increases to eliminate the excess electrolyte. If the potassium level is low, the amount of aldosterone secreted by the adrenal glands decreases.

Calcium

The balance of calcium is also regulated by the kidneys. Calcium, needed for strong bones and teeth, also plays a significant role in maintaining normal muscular contraction.

The breakdown of bones can lead to excessive calcium concentration in the extracellular fluid. As bones degenerate—perhaps as a result of bone cancer or a metabolic problem—calcium that had been trapped in bone salts is released into the plasma and interstitial fluid. A high calcium concentration can cause gastrointestinal problems such as bloating, constipation, nausea, and vomiting. Other symptoms may include poor reflexes and a lack of energy. Heart rate and blood pressure may also increase. In extreme cases, excess calcium can disrupt heart rhythms.

Calcium deficiency, on the other hand, is usually caused by a lack of calcium in the diet or by poor absorption of calcium from the intestine into the bloodstream. Because absorption is promoted by vitamin D, the problem can sometimes be linked to a deficiency of this vitamin.

By causing changes in the functioning of muscle and nerve tissues, calcium deficiency can result in twitching, spasms, and, in severe instances, epilepticlike seizures. Ultimately, the heart muscle itself can be affected, leading to an abnormal heartbeat and, possibly, cardiac failure. Calcium deficiency is rarely seen in the United States.

Calcium levels are also affected by *parathyroid hormone* (PTH), secreted by the parathyroid glands in the neck. PTH is apparently released when calcium concentration in the blood is low. The hormone then hooks onto the surface of the bones and kidneys and stimulates the kidneys to produce a substance derived from vitamin D called 1,25-$(OH)_2D_3$. This latter compound encourages the small intestine to absorb calcium from the diet and works in combination with PTH to stimulate the release of calcium from the bones.

In addition, PTH and 1,25-$(OH)_2D_3$ also increase the amount of calcium that is reabsorbed from the nephrons into the bloodstream. Moreover, parathyroid hormone decreases the amount of phosphate reabsorbed from the kidneys into the bloodstream. This is important, because the body eliminates more calcium in the urine when phosphate levels in the bloodstream are high, and eliminates less calcium when the phosphate concentration is low.

ACID-BASE BALANCE

In addition to regulating the body's electrolyte balances, the kidneys also play an important role in the regulation of *acids* and *bases*. The concept of acids and bases can be understood best by examining a molecule of water. In each water molecule, one H particle and one OH particle are held together as H-OH by a chemical bond. Sometimes that bond breaks and releases free Hs and OHs into the solution. When this happens, the H carries a positive (+) electrical charge, and is called a *hydrogen ion*. The OH carries a negative (-) electrical charge, and is referred to as a *hydroxyl radical*. For every molecule of water that breaks apart, one H^+ and one OH^- are released.

It is the relative amount of H^+ and OH^- in a solution that determines its acid-base balance. When there is an equal concentration of H^+ and OH^-, the solution is said to be neutral, with a *pH* (measure of acidity) of 7. If there is an excess of H^+ ions, the mixture is *acidic* with a pH of less than 7. If there is an excess of OH^- or too little H^+, the solution is *alkaline*, or *basic*, with a pH greater than 7. Normally, body fluids have a pH of 7.35 to 7.45—just slightly alkaline. A substantial deviation from this narrow range can have harmful consequences.

Typically, if the pH in the body becomes acidic (a condition known as *acidosis*), both *hyperkalemia* (excessive concentration of potassium) and *hypercalcemia* (exessive concentration of calcium) will

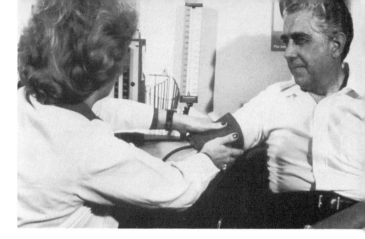

A man has his blood pressure checked. High blood pressure can result from too much sodium in the bloodstream. The kidneys play an important role in keeping sodium levels normal by helping the body eliminate sodium and retain water.

follow. In addition to these electrolyte imbalances and the symptoms that usually accompany them, the central nervous system, which comprises the brain and spinal cord, will be depressed. At the extreme, delirium and coma can develop.

In cases of acidosis, the kidneys respond to restore homeostasis. Within 24 hours of the onset of the problem, the nephrons respond by eliminating excessive acid and conserving base, thereby returning the pH to a normal level. The hydrogen can be eliminated in several ways, including as H^+, as part of an *ammonium* ion, in combination with sodium and phosphate, or as part of a *bicarbonate* molecule.

In cases of *alkalosis*, there can be too much hydroxyl radical or too little hydrogen ion in the body. In either case, the pH of the body fluids would rise above 7.45. Most often caused by *hyperventilation* (an abnormal increase in the respiratory rate), symptoms of alkalosis include numb and tingling fingers, light-headedness, arrhythmia, and muscle spasms. Once again, the kidneys serve to moderate the pH change in several ways. One method is for the kidneys to reduce the amount of ammonia formed in the nephrons. This prevents H^+ from combining with these molecules to form ammonium, and thus permits the hydrogen ions to be reabsorbed into the bloodstream. Hydrogen ions can also be released from the molecule ($H_2PO_4^-$)—formed from H^+ and phosphate—again allowing the hydrogen ions to be reabsorbed from the nephron.

NITROGEN WASTES

When food is consumed, the body must first break it down into molecules that are small enough to pass from the intestinal tract into the bloodstream. Carbohydrates are digested into simple sugars; fats are converted into fatty acids and glycerol; and proteins are broken down into amino acids.

Once these nutrients enter the bloodstream, they are usually carried to the liver for processing. There, excess nutrients are stored in various forms. Simple sugars that are not immediately needed for energy are converted either into the starch known as *glycogen* or into fats. Glycogen remains in the liver, whereas fats are stored in deposits throughout the body. Amino acids, on the other hand, are normally used to manufacture protein in the body. If excess protein is available, it will be converted to fats for storage in the liver.

When the cells require food for energy, the nutrients are mobilized, often in the liver, and sent throughout the body via the bloodstream. As mentioned earlier, the simple sugar glucose is the primary cellular food. When energy needs must be met, long molecules of glycogen are broken down into glucose in the liver and then released into the bloodstream. Fats are the next most common cellular nutrient. When needed, fat molecules are brought to the liver, and broken down into glycerol and fatty acids. Whereas the fatty acids are reduced to ketone bodies (eliminated in the urine), glycerol is converted into glucose for cellular use.

Proteins are the least used cellular nutrient. Because protein is the major component of body muscle, weakness and wasting may occur when protein is released from muscle into the bloodstream for fuel. If the body is starving, however, protein is broken down into amino acids and brought to the liver for processing. Here the amino (nitrogen-containing) fragment of the amino acid is removed. The remaining amino acid fragment can then be converted to glucose, while the nitrogen component is changed into urea. Urea, in turn, is a major nitrogen waste eliminated by the kidneys. Other nitrogen wastes excreted by the renal system include uric acid, *creatine*, and *creatinine*. When renal failure occurs, these nitrogen wastes, which are toxic to the body, accumulate in the bloodstream. Irreversible kidney failure results in death, unless the patient undergoes dialysis or a transplant.

CHAPTER 3

KIDNEY FUNCTION

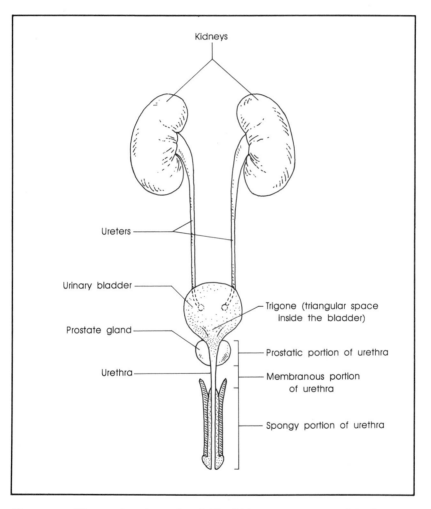

Kidneys

Ureters

Urinary bladder

Trigone (triangular space inside the bladder)

Prostate gland

Prostatic portion of urethra

Urethra

Membranous portion of urethra

Spongy portion of urethra

Diagram of the male urinary tract. The kidneys are responsible for filtering fluid out of the bloodstream, retaining what is needed in the body and sending the rest through the tract to be eliminated as urine.

The kidney is a bean-shaped organ consisting of an outer *cortex* and an inner *medulla*. Looking at a cross section of the medulla, one would see triangular-shaped wedges, called *renal pyramids*, with points directed inward. From the point (*renal papilla*) of each pyramid, urine flows through an opening and into a cuplike receptacle called the *minor calyx*. The minor calyces lead into larger cavities called the *major calyces*. These, in turn, merge into a cavity called the *renal pelvis*. It is from a slit in this pelvis, called the *hilum*, that blood vessels and nerves enter and leave the kidneys, and the ureters originate to carry urine to the bladder.

NEPHRONS: ANATOMY AND FUNCTION

The kidneys are very complex structures, each containing about one million urine-producing units called nephrons. The nephrons filter fluid out of the bloodstream, process the fluid, and then retain what is needed, eliminating the rest as urine.

As previously mentioned, each nephron includes a ball of capillaries called a glomerulus sitting within another cuplike receptacle called a Bowman's capsule. Typically, during the process of filtration, pressurized fluid from the blood filters through the capillary walls into the Bowman's capsule. Actually, the fluid must pass through three layers of membrane as it leaves the capillaries. The first layer, called the *endothelium*, contains holes, or *fenestrations*, that allow water and certain other molecules to get through. Surrounding the endothelium is a second layer called the *basement membrane*, made from fibrous proteins. Just above this is the *visceral layer*, which contains openings called *filtration slits*.

The three layers together are called the *endothelial capsular membrane*. This barrier usually prevents blood cells and large protein molecules from getting through, but water, urea, electrolytes, sugars, and amino acids can pass into the Bowman's capsule.

After entering the Bowman's capsule, the fluid, or *glomerular filtrate*, continues into a small, coiled tube called the *proximal convoluted tubule* (PCT). During a normal day for an average adult, about

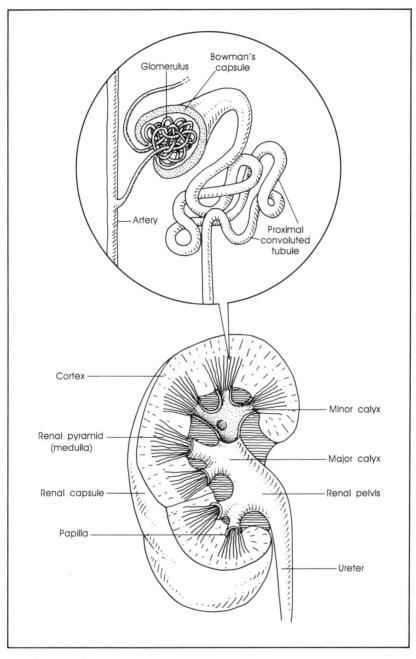

Anatomy of the kidney

380 pints of plasma filter into the nephron, yet only 2 to 4 pints of this original filtrate actually appear in the urine.

Why the discrepancy? Once in the PCT, the composition of the filtrate is modified considerably, because many substances are reabsorbed into the bloodstream as needed through a nest of blood vessels called the *peritubular capillaries*. Therefore, much or all of a variety

A detailed illustration of the internal structure of the nephron, demonstrating its complex array of components

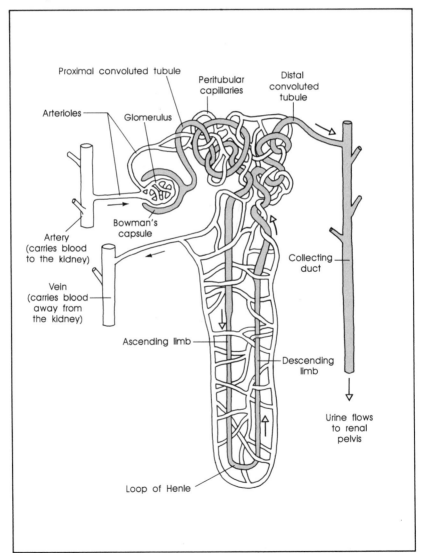

of needed substances—including water, sodium, chloride, sugar, calcium, proteins, and amino acids—are retained in the body, rather than eliminated in the urine.

From the PCT, fluid is carried through the U-shaped *loop of Henle* and on to the *distal convoluted tubule* (DCT) and *collecting duct* (CD), with more reabsorption occurring along the way. By the time urine drains into the ureters, about 99% of the original glomerular filtrate has been reabsorbed into the bloodstream.

Some substances, however, are not reabsorbed, because they would be toxic if retained in the body. Urea, uric acid, creatinine, nitrates, and potassium are usually concentrated in the tubules of the nephrons and subsequently eliminated.

eliminated substances

Tubular secretion is another process that can modify the composition of urine. In these cases, certain substances are secreted from the blood vessels surrounding the nephron directly into the DCT and CD. For example, potassium and hydrogen are secreted as necessary, to maintain homeostasis.

Active and Passive Transport

Both tubular secretion and reabsorption are accomplished through several different processes, including *active transport* and *passive transport*. In active transport, a substance such as glucose can pass from side A of a selectively permeable membrane to side B, even if the concentration of glucose on side B is already higher than on side A. (In osmosis, remember, water molecules can move only from an area of higher concentration to one of lower concentration.) For this to happen, the glucose must latch onto a protein molecule that can literally move it to the area of higher concentration. In addition, the energy in the glucose molecule is not enough to get it across the membrane. The body must supply extra energy to give it a push.

In passive transport, the molecule's own energy is enough to get it through the membrane. The body does not need to supply the extra push. Osmosis is one form of passive transport. Another is *simple diffusion*, again a process in which molecules move from an area of higher concentration to one of lower concentration.

Evolution of the Kidneys

The kidney is, universally, an excretory organ, but its design and function vary from one species to the next in accordance with the specific needs of an animal and the environment in which it lives. The kidneys of *vertebrates*—that is, fish, amphibians, reptiles, birds, and mammals, all of whom possess a vertebral column—will be considered here.

Primitive marine animals probably did not need an advanced mechanism to conserve or eliminate water because their body fluid was no more concentrated than the water in which they lived. When they eventually moved into fresh water, however, they were in danger of taking in too much liquid through osmosis because their body fluid contained a higher sodium concentration than the fresh water they inhabited. (As previously explained, water will pass through a selectively permeable membrane from an area of higher concentration to one of lower concentration.) Therefore, these animals needed to develop kidneys in order to remove excess water.

Later, some of these creatures evolved into land-dwelling animals or returned to salt water (even though by this time they had developed blood that was less concentrated than their ocean environment). Their primary concern was now to conserve water rather than excrete it, and their kidneys had to change accordingly. As a result, some marine fish today have no glomeruli to filter water into the kidney, although some amount of water is secreted elsewhere along the nephron. In other ocean-dwelling fish, the size of the glomeruli has been reduced.

Despite their variations, the kidneys of all vertebrates contain nephrons. However, the kidneys of a small fish may have a few dozen nephrons, compared to the approximately 1 million nephrons found in each human kidney. Although some fish do not have glomeruli, these structures occur in the kidneys of most vertebrates. The majority of vertebrates, therefore, produce urine through the filtration-reabsorption method, in which water and other substances are filtered through the glomeruli and then, to a large extent, reabsorbed back into the bloodstream as these products move through the nephron. One advantage to this type of kidney is that it provides a more flexible system for eliminating toxic substances, giving an animal a greater ability to adapt to unfamiliar environments, which may contain potentially dangerous substances. Fish that possess kidneys with no glomeruli tend to live in stable environments, which require no such ability to adapt.

In the nephron, the loop of Henle plays an essential role in the production of a highly concentrated urine—that is, urine that contains a higher concentration of various products, such as sodium, than the blood does. However, the loop of Henle is not found in the nephrons of fish, amphibians, and reptiles, and as a result, these animals cannot produce urine that has any greater concentration of dissolved substances in it than their blood.

This arrangement is fine for freshwater animals because they are more concerned with eliminating excess water than with conserving fluid. For marine fish, however, this dilute urine is not an adequate means of eliminating the large amounts of salt they take in. Therefore, they eliminate excess salt through their gills.

The loop of Henle is found in birds and mammals, which means that both of these animals can manufacture highly concentrated urine. As a result, they can conserve water by allowing waste products to build up in their urine before releasing it, instead of having to urinate frequently to eliminate toxic substances.

Reptiles also have means of conserving water. Rather than excreting urea, they eliminate much of their waste in the form of crystals made from uric acid, which can be swept from the body using relatively little water. Birds also use this method.

EXITING THE KIDNEYS

As discussed, urine exits the kidneys, flows through the ureters, and enters the bladder for storage. The bladder normally contains about half a pint of urine but can expand to hold more than three and a half pints if necessary. When a woman is pregnant, the expanding uterus pushes down on the bladder and prevents it from filling completely. This reduction of the normal capacity of the bladder explains why pregnant women urinate frequently.

This diagram illustrates the steps involved in the formation of urine in the nephron. The drawing is highly simplified, and the appearance of some of the components of the nephron have been altered for the sake of clarity.

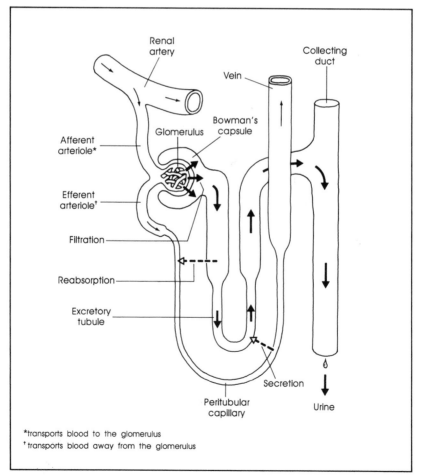

*transports blood to the glomerulus
† transports blood away from the glomerulus

When the bladder becomes full, messages are sent to the spinal cord, and a feeling of urgency results. A band-shaped *sphincter muscle* at the neck of the urethra allows an individual to control urination. This muscle relaxes when the brain gives the "okay," and, as the bladder walls contract, urine is pushed through the urethra and out of the body.

During infancy, the brain and spinal cord are apparently not mature enough to mediate control over the release of urine—hence, the need for diapers. A problem can also arise in people who have sustained damage to the nervous system and are thus rendered *incontinent* (unable to voluntarily control urination).

Although the urethra performs the same basic function in the male and the female, there are some differences worthy of mention. The urethra is about one and a half inches long in the female and serves only to eliminate urine. Its short length and the proximity of its opening to that of the anus are believed to account for the frequency of urinary tract and bladder infections in women. The male urethra is approximately seven to eight inches long and carries both urine and sperm. Because urine is harmful to sperm, the male's system is designed to minimize contact between urine and *seminal fluid* (the fluid that carries sperm). Doctors refer to three separate sections of the male urethra, corresponding to the three areas of the body through which it passes. The *prostatic portion* of the urethra travels through the prostate gland; the *membranous portion* passes through the *pelvic diaphragm* (a muscular wall that supports such organs as the bladder and rectum); and the *spongy portion* runs the length of the penis.

HORMONES AND URINE PRODUCTION

The formation of urine is a very complicated process that must be well orchestrated. There are two chemicals in the plasma that together play an important role in mediating appropriate reabsorption and secretion of substances into and out of the nephrons. These are the hormones aldosterone, and *antidiuretic hormone* (ADH).

The role of aldosterone was discussed in Chapter 2. The other hormone, ADH, is released from the pituitary gland, located at the base of the brain, and promotes water reabsorption from the DCT and CD of the nephron. Without ADH, a high percentage of fluid that had

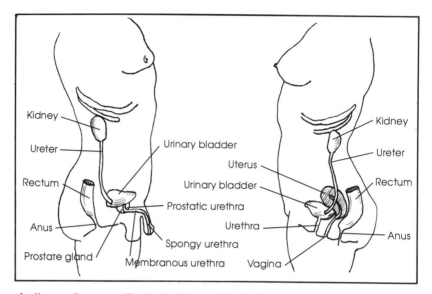

As these diagrams illustrate, the urethra is shorter in women than in men. In addition, the proximity of the opening of the female urethra to the anus may account for the frequency of urinary tract and bladder infections in women.

originally filtered into the Bowman's capsule from the glomerulus would be lost in urine, and significant dehydration would result.

DRUGS AND URINE FORMATION

When an individual is retaining too much water, it is sometimes possible to stimulate fluid loss with diuretics. These medications are commonly used when excessive fluid retention aggravates existing medical conditions, such as high blood pressure and heart disease.

The mode of action of diuretics is varied. Some inhibit the action of aldosterone. Other diuretics work by decreasing the secretion of ADH. One diuretic that does the latter is, oddly enough, water, when ingested in large quantities. If body fluids are diluted by water, ADH output is automatically depressed. Because ADH is essential to the reabsorption of water, a reduction in the hormone causes increased urination. In fact, many weight-loss programs recommend the consumption of at least eight glasses of water per day. Another diuretic that inhibits ADH secretion and increases urine output is alcohol. This effect accounts for the dry mouth and heavy head usually experienced the morning after an evening of excessive alcohol consumption.

CHAPTER 4

CAUSES OF KIDNEY DISEASE

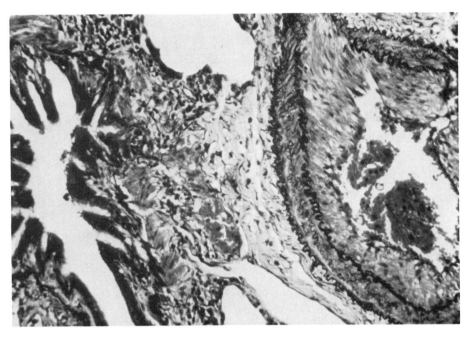

Microscopic photograph of a renal blood vessel

Because of their central role in homeostasis, the kidneys are essential to good health. For this reason, kidney disease often has life-threatening consequences. Kidney disorders can originate from a variety of sources, including infection (which will be discussed in Chapter 5), obstruction of the urinary tract, circulation problems, metabolic disorders, and toxic substances.

OBSTRUCTION OF THE URINARY TRACT

Sometimes an obstruction interferes with the movement of fluid through the urinary tract. Several types of blockage can occur, including kidney stones, scars in the ureter, an enlarged prostate gland (in males), a narrowing or blockage of the urethra (from scarring caused by injury or chronic inflammation), and tumors in the urinary tract.

If the blockage occurs between the kidney and the bladder, it can cause fluid and pressure to build up in the renal pelvis and ureters. This buildup may result in a condition called *hydronephrosis*, in which the renal pelvis enlarges and the nephrons may be destroyed.

This type of blockage can also lead to *pyelonephritis*, an infection of the kidneys. Ordinarily, the flushing action of urine helps to wash out bacteria that might otherwise contaminate the urinary tract. When fluid becomes stagnant and does not drain properly, the potential for infection increases.

Similar symptoms may evolve when there is an obstruction in the urethra. A blockage can cause urine to flow back up into the ureters. This reverse flow often carries bacteria with it, causing an infection to develop.

CIRCULATION AND KIDNEY FUNCTION

Like all cells of the body, kidney cells must receive an adequate blood supply to survive. Otherwise, they will die from lack of oxygen, nutrients, and adequate waste removal. However, there are a number of reasons why the volume of blood circulating through the body—and to the kidneys—will decrease. Severe burns, hemorrhaging, and excessive vomiting, for example, all cause fluid loss, diminishing the amount of plasma in the blood.

Hypertension

By the same token, too much blood flowing through the kidneys can also pose a danger, as seen in people with untreated *hypertension*, or high blood pressure. A major problem in the United States, it is estimated that hypertension affects more than 61 million Americans, according to the American Heart Association, yet doctors often cannot pinpoint the cause. As hypertension develops, the blood pushes with greater and greater force against the walls of the arteries, and this, over time, can damage the blood vessels, including those in the heart, brain, and kidneys. The result can be heart disease, stroke, and kidney failure.

Renal Artery Stenosis

Renal artery stenosis occurs when the artery supplying the kidney is abnormally narrowed, preventing the renal cells from getting the oxygen and nutrients they need to survive. The narrowing may be caused by fibrous tissue that invades the artery or by a *congenital* condition (one that is present at birth).

The affected kidney responds to the lack of blood by releasing renin, an enzyme that, as previously discussed, ultimately stimulates an increase in blood pressure. In this case, however, hypertension can result, with the pressure going dangerously high. This increase in pressure will not harm the affected kidney because, as a result of the narrowed artery, it will not receive an excessive amount of blood. However, the other kidney can be damaged.

Renal artery stenosis can be corrected via surgery or through *angioplasty*, a technique in which doctors expand the narrowed artery space using a tube with a balloon at the tip.

METABOLIC DISORDERS

Kidney disease sometimes results from metabolic disorders. Patients with *diabetes mellitus*—a disease that prevents the body from properly using sugars and starches—also tend to have destructive changes in small blood vessels throughout the body. The two organs most critically affected are the eyes and the kidneys. In the kidneys, the changes cause arteriosclerosis and damage to the *arterioles* (small, branching arteries that transport blood to the capillaries), glomeruli, and renal papillae.

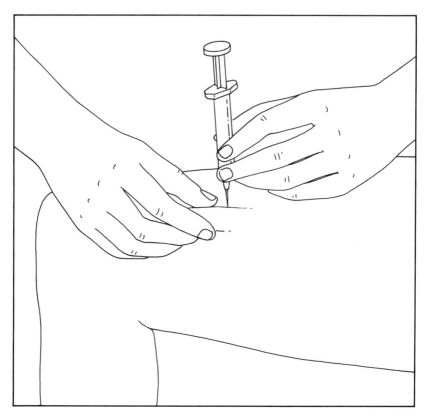

Diabetes can be controlled through insulin injections to regulate blood sugar levels. The disease can cause destructive changes in small blood vessels throughout the body, particularly in the eyes and the kidneys.

Gout, another metabolic disorder, can also lead to kidney trouble. The excess uric acid that characterizes this disease is deposited in the fluids and tissues of the body. Common sites for uric acid accumulation are the joints and the kidneys, and renal buildup can result in kidney failure.

A tumor in the parathyroid glands can also affect renal function. By triggering the release of excess parathyroid hormone, the tumor can cause a dramatic increase in calcium levels in the blood. As a result, calcium salts deposit in the soft tissue of the kidneys, leading, if unchecked, to renal failure.

TOXIC SUBSTANCES

Toxic substances can have a variety of harmful effects. Some cause cardiac arrest, others paralyze the muscles of respiration (breathing), and some can damage or destroy the kidneys. At times, products that are toxic and can cause renal damage are used by uninformed people who have no understanding of how poisonous these substances are.

The pain-killing drug phenacetin, for example, can be harmful if used excessively or over a long period. People who suffer from constant headaches, and hypochondriacs with many imagined pains are particularly likely to become abusers. But overusing this drug can lead to renal failure.

Carbon tetrachloride, commonly used in dry-cleaning fluid, is also toxic to the kidneys. The chemical poses a particular danger to individuals who have consumed alcoholic beverages. The combination of carbon tetrachloride fumes with ethyl alcohol in the bloodstream leads to the formation of a substance that is severely poisonous to the kidneys.

Parathyroid hormone, released by the parathyroid glands in the neck, affects the amount of calcium in the bloodstream. A tumor in the glands can trigger the release of excess parathyroid hormone, resulting in a dangerous accumulation of calcium salts in the kidneys.

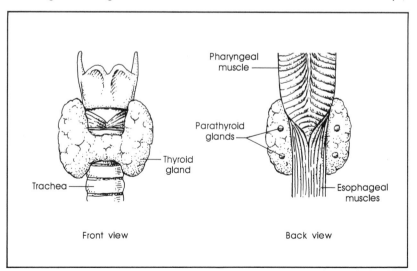

Pharyngeal muscle

Parathyroid glands

Thyroid gland

Trachea

Esophageal muscles

Front view

Back view

Lead can also cause renal damage. Eliminated from paints, where it was once a standard ingredient, lead can still be found in illegally distilled whiskey. Once in the body, it tends to accumulate in bones as well as in the cells of the nephron. Damage usually occurs slowly, ultimately leading to renal failure.

Ironically, some medications that are normally useful in combating a variety of diseases may also damage the kidneys. These medications include certain antibiotics and two drugs frequently used to treat rheumatoid arthritis, gold and penicillamine.

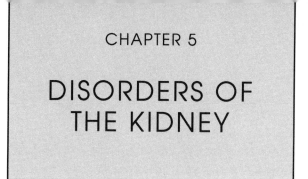

CHAPTER 5

DISORDERS OF THE KIDNEY

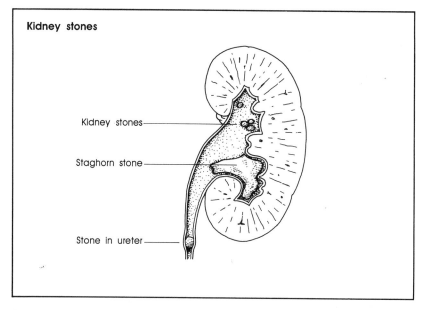

Kidney stones

Kidney stones

Staghorn stone

Stone in ureter

Kidney stones often cause severe pain. If a stone blocks the urinary tract and prevents wastes from being eliminated, kidney infection may result.

There are many causes of kidney disease. As discussed in Chapter 4, obstruction, changes in blood flow, metabolic disorders, and toxins may all play a part. This chapter will continue to examine factors affecting kidney function, including such common disorders as congenital and hereditary abnormalities, kidney stones, pyelonephritis, and *glomerulonephritis*.

CONGENITAL AND HEREDITARY ABNORMALITIES

Although congenital abnormalities are present at birth, they are not necessarily caused by a genetic mutation passed from parent to child. Toxins or other factors can be the source. Hereditary abnormalities, on the other hand, are passed genetically from one generation to the next.

A congenital abnormality may involve anything from the number of kidneys a person has to the location of these organs in the body. If a baby is born with one kidney instead of two, survival is possible as long as the existing organ remains functional. In rare instances an individual is born with more than two kidneys. Sometimes discovered by accident, this condition does not usually cause renal problems.

Ectopic (poorly positioned) kidneys are another congenital abnormality. In some cases, the kidneys are located in the chest cavity. Pain results as the kidneys crowd the lungs and heart, pressing on nerves and soft tissue in the area. Sometimes both kidneys are found on the same side of the body, a condition usually discovered accidentally when an X-ray examination of the abdominal cavity is performed.

Polycystic kidney disease is a hereditary disorder characterized by the formation of a number of grapelike cysts within the kidney. In most cases polycystic disease does not become a problem until sometime between the ages of 20 and 50. When cysts appear, symptoms include a dull ache in the lower back and blood in the urine. High blood pressure occurs in 50% or more of such cases. Often the kidneys become greatly enlarged, and over time (typically as long as 16 years), as healthy kidney is replaced by cysts and fibrous tissue, renal failure results.

Because there is no known cure for this disorder, treatment often focuses on preventing kidney infection and controlling associated hypertension. Polycystic patients tend to be good candidates for dialysis and kidney transplant because the disease rarely affects other organs.

In rare cases the disease may appear in infancy. The outlook for a baby born with *infantile polycystic kidney disease* is poor, and many such children die shortly after birth. However, a kidney transplant may improve the infant's chances of survival.

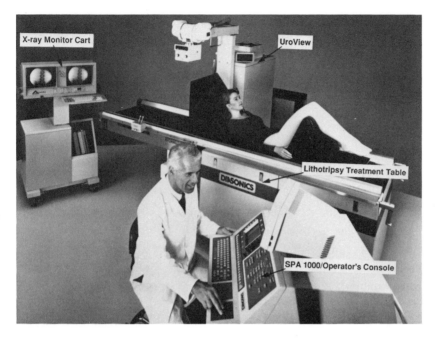

Through the technique known as extracorporeal shock wave litho-tripsy, high-energy shock waves are used to pulverize kidney stones so that they can be eliminated in the urine.

KIDNEY STONES

It has been estimated that in the United States more than 200,000 people are admitted into the hospital each year because of kidney stones. This figure does not include cases that require no hospitalization, or instances in which treatment is administered in emergency rooms or in clinics.

Stones are believed to develop when substances in the urine form crystals that cling together. About 65% of stones are formed from a combination of calcium oxalate and calcium phosphate. Uric acid, magnesium ammonium phosphate, and cystine (an amino acid) are also found in some stones. Kidney stones are usually only a fraction of an inch in diameter, and the surface may be smooth or jagged. Sometimes, however, a stone grows to fill in the hollow spaces of the renal pelvis, giving the stone a *staghorn* shape.

Although the exact reason for stone formation is not clearly understood, there are a number of factors that encourage the development of renal calculi. If substances such as calcium or uric acid reach too high a level in the bloodstream, there is a tendency for them to *precipitate* (condense and separate from the liquid) as crystals. If, for example, an individual becomes dehydrated, the amount of fluid in the urine can drop, so that stone-forming substances in it become unusually concentrated.

Excessive calcium in the blood can result from bone degeneration that releases calcium into the bloodstream, from excessive absorption of calcium from the gastrointestinal tract (which can result from overactive parathyroid glands), or from increased reabsorption of calcium from the kidneys. More often, however, the amount of calcium in the blood is normal but, for unknown reasons, calcium levels in the urine are high, leading to the formation of stones.

Some substances that normally exist in urine tend to inhibit stone formation, including citrate, a form of citric acid. In the absence of such substances, more crystals will deposit.

Anything interfering with the flow of urine, such as scar tissue in the urinary tract, can also encourage stones to develop. This happens because crystals precipitate more readily in stagnant fluid.

Uric acid stones are commonly noted in patients with gout, as a result of high uric acid concentration in the bloodstream. A connection also seems to exist between kidney stones and high levels of protein in the diet. It may be that protein encourages stones to develop by stimulating the excretion of uric acid, phosphorous, and calcium into the urine. Usually, however, physicians cannot pinpoint exactly why kidney stones develop.

Regardless of the type of stone, symptoms of renal calculi are similar. There is often severe pain—known as *renal colic*—particularly when the stones shift in the urinary tract. Kidney stones can also irritate the lining and tubes of the kidney, resulting in blood in the urine. Moreover, if a stone blocks the flow of urine, the kidney may become infected.

Much of the time, renal stones are passed out of the body through the urine. If the stones are small enough to be eliminated this way,

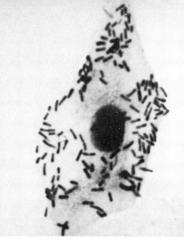

Microscopic view of bacteria in the urinary tract. These organisms can cause the kidney infection known as pyelonephritis.

patients are usually instructed to drink large amounts of fluids, because drinking encourages urination and may help flush the calculi from the system.

If all else fails, surgery is sometimes necessary. Whenever possible, however, high-energy shock waves are now used by physicians to break stones into tiny particles that can then be eliminated in the urine. This technique, extracorporeal shock wave lithotripsy, costs less and requires a shorter recovery time than does surgery. However, the procedure cannot be used on all types of stones, and it sometimes leaves fragments behind.

About 25% of the time stones will recur unless preventive measures are taken. Usually stones reappear within 2 to 3 years after the first attack, but they may also recur 20 to 30 years later. Because it is impossible to predict who will or will not have repeat episodes of renal calculi, some preventive measures are generally recommended for all kidney stone patients. Prevention includes an increase in fluid intake to help dilute stone-forming substances in the urine. A patient also may be advised to restrict the amount of protein in his or her diet as well as the amount of salt (salt encourages the excretion of calcium into the urine).

PYELONEPHRITIS

Pyelonephritis is a bacterial infection of the kidney. Most often this disorder develops when bacteria travel up the urethra to the bladder. If a defect in the urinary tract, such as a faulty valve between the bladder and the ureter, allows some of the infected urine to flow back up to the kidney (an action known as *reflux*), pyelonephritis can result. Bacteria can also be carried to the kidneys through the bloodstream.

Common symptoms of pyelonephritis are a frequent, urgent need to urinate and a burning sensation during urination. Other symptoms include fever, chills, and nausea, and the urine is usually cloudy, bloody, and filled with bacteria.

The disease is usually treated with antibiotics. Without proper care, the infection may recur frequently and develop into a chronic condition. Eventually it can lead to destruction of the nephrons, which are then replaced with scar tissue. The kidneys become smaller and less functional, and renal failure ultimately sets in.

GLOMERULONEPHRITIS

Glomerulonephritis is a kidney disease characterized by damage to the glomerulus of the nephron. *Acute* (severe, but short-lived) *postinfectious glomerulonephritis* may occur after a bacterial or viral infection. The initial infection may be mumps, chicken pox, measles, malaria, or, quite commonly, *streptococcal* infections of the throat or skin. (Streptococci are a type of bacterium.)

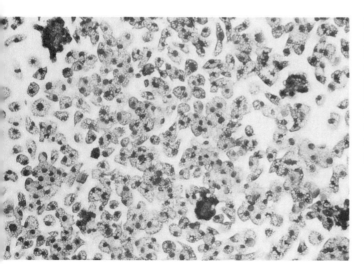

Microscopic view of white blood cells used by the immune system against disease; in glomerulonephritis, the immune response backfires, causing inflammation of the glomeruli and destroying glomerular tissue.

In response to the infection, the immune system attacks the invading agents. Sometimes, however, the immune mechanism backfires, causing severe inflammation in the glomeruli of the nephrons and destroying glomerular tissue. This disorder most commonly affects children and young adults, and usually there is a complete recovery.

Symptoms of acute glomerulonephritis include fever, chills, weakness, nausea, and vomiting. One very telling sign is edema—the swelling associated with water retention. Because glomerulonephritis damages the capillary membranes of the glomerulus, large protein molecules and blood can leak into the nephron and subsequently be eliminated in the urine. (The blood, consequently, can turn urine dark.) Protein ordinarily helps to maintain the fluid balance in the body, so its loss results in the accumulation of excess fluid in the interstitial spaces. Fluid retention then causes a variety of problems, including high blood pressure and excess fluid in the lungs. *Hypertensive encephalopathy*, a condition caused by high blood pressure in the brain, can also occur, leading to seizures and possible loss of clear vision as a result of swelling of the *retina* (the layer of the eyeball that contains the nerve cells sensitive to light stimulation).

The chronic form of glomerulonephritis may develop from many different diseases, such as acute glomerulonephritis that fails to disappear. Often the patient has no noticeable symptoms of chronic glomerulonephritis for a number of years, while the kidney becomes increasingly scarred from the disease. As in pyelonephritis, it takes on a granular, pitted appearance. When symptoms ultimately do appear, protein loss and subsequent edema may become so severe that the sufferer's eyes swell shut. Excess fluid also causes increased pressure in the brain, chest, and around the heart. Chronic glomerulonephritis is the most common culprit behind permanent, irreversible failure of both kidneys.

Unfortunately, glomerulonephritis can be difficult to prevent because streptococcal infections of the throat are themselves hard to avoid. But prompt treatment of streptococcal infections may reduce the chance of kidney disease. Various medications, including steroids, have been used against chronic glomerulonephritis but with only limited success.

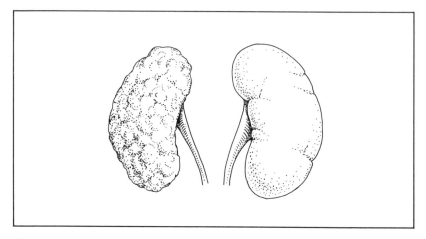

Chronic glomerulonephritis can destroy kidney tissue, giving the organ a granular, pitted texture, as represented by the drawing on the left.

WARNING SIGNS OF KIDNEY DISEASE

The National Kidney Foundation provides a list of the warning signs of kidney disease. These include

- puffy eyes, particularly in children;
- gradual swelling, a problem that will commonly occur in the ankles;
- pain in the lower back area just below the rib cage;
- changes in the pattern of urination (such as more trips to the bathroom at night) or an increased frequency of urination in general;
- urinary difficulties, including painful urination or the appearance of blood in the urine; and
- high blood pressure.

DIAGNOSING KIDNEY DISEASE

Urinalysis

Many a patient has gone into a doctor's office and been handed a specimen cup to be filled with urine. Why is this procedure done so frequently? Because urinalysis is a good starting point for the diagnosis of many problems. A physician can learn much about the hidden physiological workings of the body by examining the urine with respect to glucose, protein, blood, ketone bodies, pH, concentration of electrolytes, and bacteria. Although a urinalysis is merely an early step in the examination process, it can be a significant factor in leading a physician to a correct diagnosis.

Often, abnormal urine is not a reflection of disease in the kidney, but rather an indication of a problem elsewhere in the body. Glucose in the urine, for example, is the result of excessive glucose in the bloodstream. Normally, glucose is filtered from the glomerulus into the Bowman's capsule and then reabsorbed back into the bloodstream from the PCT. If glucose appears in the urine, it is because too much glucose is being filtered into the nephrons to be reabsorbed fully into the tubules and hence is spilled out in the urine.

The most common cause of this problem is uncontrolled diabetes mellitus. Because a person with diabetes cannot properly utilize sugars and starches, glucose, a building block of these substances, remains dissolved in plasma while the cells starve for nourishment. Diabetics are often asked to check for glucose in their urine to see if the disease is being adequately controlled. Dipsticks used for this purpose are available at pharmacies.

Other substances that appear abnormally in the blood and urine as a result of diabetes are ketone bodies such as *acetone* and *acetoacetic acid*. These chemicals are produced when cells are forced to burn fats instead of sugars to meet their metabolic needs, a reaction that occurs, for example, in cases of severe malnutrition or starvation and some high-protein diets.

The pH of the urine can reflect certain metabolic or physiological problems. In the healthy adult, this pH ranges between 4.5 and 8.0, but it is most commonly measured at 6.0. A persistently alkaline urine, however, could indicate a urinary tract infection, potassium depletion, or *renal tubular acidosis* (a kidney disease characterized by an inability to retain alkaline substances). Ketones, on the other hand, will acidify the urine and cause the pH to fall.

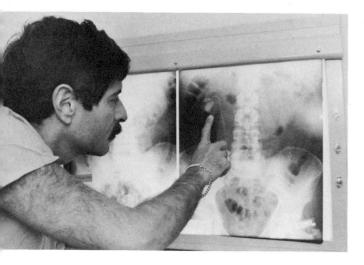

A kidney stone is viewed on an X ray.

The pH of the urine is also known to affect the formation of kidney stones, with calculi most likely forming in either an acidic or alkaline environment, depending on the materials making up the stones.

Other Diagnostic Procedures

Along with urinalysis, there are other ways to determine whether the kidneys are functioning adequately. One commonly used test is a *clearance study*—a measure of how long it takes for a specific amount of some substance, such as urea, to be removed by the kidneys from a given amount of plasma.

The formula for figuring out the plasma clearance rate is: **The number of milligrams of the substance excreted by the kidneys into the urine per minute** divided by **the number of milligrams of the substance per milliliter of plasma**. This means that if, for example, a person's blood plasma contains a concentration of 2 milligrams of substance A per milliliter, and the kidneys excrete 4 milligrams of substance A per minute, then the plasma clearance rate of substance A is: **4 milligrams per minute/2 milligrams per milliliter**, or **2 milliliters per minute**.

The plasma clearance rate of a substance provides a rough idea of the kidney's *glomerular filtration rate*, or the amount of fluid per minute that filters through the capillary walls of the glomerulus into the Bowman's capsule. The higher the glomerular filtration rate, the faster a substance will be removed from the plasma, and therefore, the higher that substance's plasma clearance rate will be. If the normal plasma clearance rate for substance A is 2 milliliters per minute, but a physician finds that a patient's clearance rate is only 1 milliliter per minute, the test indicates that the patient's glomerular filtration rate is abnormally low and that he or she may be suffering from a kidney disorder.

Another diagnostic technique is *cystoscopy*, in which an instrument called a *cystoscope* is inserted through the urethra to examine the interior of the bladder and ureters. Cystoscopy provides a means to inspect tumors, stones, and ulcers, to collect urine from the renal pelvis, and to measure bladder capacity.

Additional information can be derived from radiological studies, such as X rays and intravenous pyelograms (IVPs). An X ray of the kidneys, ureters, and bladder can help identify soft tissue masses and certain renal stones. An intravenous pyelogram involves the injection of a *radiopaque* (impenetrable to X rays or other forms of radiation) dye into the urinary tract, followed by an X ray. This procedure enables the physician to observe the location, size, and configuration of the organs in the urinary tract and to identify abnormalities.

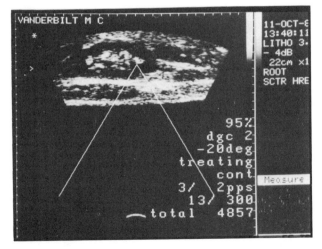

This ultrasound image, produced by sound waves reflected off the inside of the body, has been used to locate a kidney stone.

Ultrasound tests are also used in the diagnosis of kidney disorders. In this procedure, ultra-high-frequency sound waves are reflected off of the kidney, producing an image of the organ. Ultrasound can be used to determine the size, shape, and consistency of the kidneys, ureters, and bladder, and can aid in the detection of polycystic kidney disease.

Color

The color of a patient's urine can also play a role in diagnosis. Although foods sometimes cause a color change—blackberries, rhubarb, and beets may give urine a red tint—color can also be an indication of injury or disease.

A reddish brown or tea-colored urine, for example, can result from release of protein from damaged muscle. Most often, though, red urine is caused by bleeding in the urinary tract. The tint tends to be either dark red or "cola color" if the blood comes from the upper tract, and brighter red when it originates in the lower tract. Blood in the urine may be an early sign of a bladder infection, or *cystitis*.

CHAPTER 6

KIDNEY FAILURE

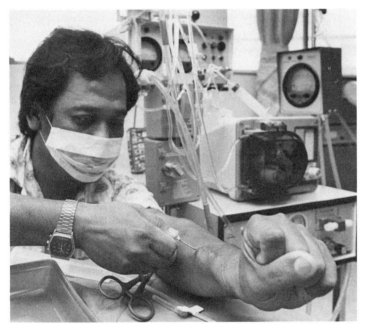

A patient connects himself to a dialysis machine.

The onset of kidney failure can vary from sudden (acute renal failure) to slow and long-term (chronic renal failure). In either case, as toxic wastes accumulate in the bloodstream and homeostasis is destroyed, the physiological consequences can be devastating.

ACUTE RENAL FAILURE

Causes

In acute renal failure the kidneys stop working suddenly and completely. This often results when a major surgical operation sends the body into shock, depriving the kidneys of blood. Shock resulting from severe injury or other causes can also lead to acute failure.

Acute glomerulonephritis can also cause acute kidney failure. Usually the inflammation caused by glomerulonephritis subsides and normal kidney function returns within several weeks to a few months. But if too many glomeruli have been destroyed, chronic renal failure may develop.

Damage to or destruction of the tubules in the nephrons can also cause acute renal failure. Renal toxins such as carbon tetrachloride, cadmium, and heavy metals are especially destructive to the tubule cells of the nephron. When damaged, these cells frequently slough off and plug up the tubule. This blockage interferes with normal functioning of the kidneys, but new cells usually grow within 10 to 20 days, and the damage is repaired.

Another problem that inevitably affects the kidneys is a *transfusion reaction*. If a person receives a transfusion from someone with an incompatible blood type, the incoming red blood cells are destroyed by antibodies in the recipient's blood. Destruction leads to leakage of *hemoglobin* (the red protein pigment within the red blood cell that carries oxygen) and its subsequent passage into the nephron. This leakage, in turn, blocks the kidney tubules, and renal function may cease.

Symptoms

The symptoms of acute renal failure are wide-ranging. Urine output falls to a pint or less per day, allowing metabolic waste products, acids, and potassium to accumulate in the bloodstream. Excess potassium can interfere with cardiac contraction, causing an irregular heartbeat and, in some cases, heart failure. Fluid and sodium retention may result in

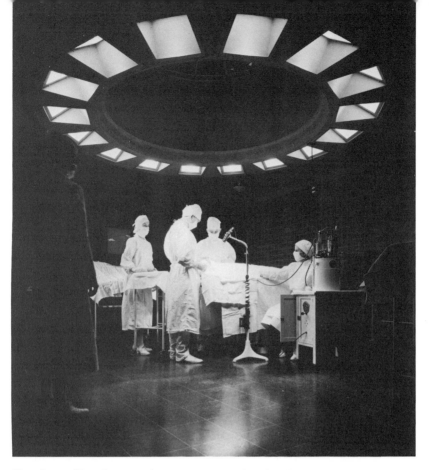

Shock resulting from major surgery can deprive the kidneys of blood, causing acute renal failure.

edema of the face and extremities, high blood pressure, accumulation of fluid in the heart and lungs, and ultimately, heart failure, resulting from fluid overload. (The effects of renal failure will be more fully explored later in the chapter.)

A patient with these symptoms can be treated with medication or dialysis. The first stage of improvement usually involves an increase in urine output to more than a pint per day. This period usually lasts two to three weeks. During that time, sodium and potassium may be washed out in the urine. Ultimately, the tubule cells recover sufficiently to reabsorb sodium and potassium and eliminate metabolic wastes. Total recovery takes up to a year or more, and sometimes the kidneys are left with a legacy of problems caused by the damaged nephrons.

Psychological Aspects of Dialysis

Researchers have found that a dialysis patient's mental attitude also plays an important role in successful treatment of renal disease. One study, for example, indicates that the amount of moral support an individual receives from family members and medical personnel can affect that patient's compliance with certain dietary restrictions. For unknown reasons, age and gender also appear to have an effect.

Patients suffering from chronic kidney failure must stick to a health regimen that includes proper nutrition. For example, these individuals must limit the amount of phosphorous in their diet because the kidneys are unable to eliminate the excess. (Large amounts of phosphorous are found in milk, cheese, nuts, and peas.) Patients can also take aluminum hydroxide gel, which latches onto phosphorous in the digestive tract and prevents it from being absorbed by the body. Potassium can also reach unhealthy levels, so that patients must avoid eating too much potassium-rich food, such as meat, nuts, milk, fruits, and vegetables.

A study published in the *Journal of Applied Social Psychology* (December 1990) looked at 60 hemodialysis patients (Hemodialysis is defined in Chapter 7.) The researchers examined how well the people around each patient helped the patient meet his or her needs and also how well these people helped the patient maintain a feeling of self-worth.

The researchers found that dialysis patients who did not believe that they were receiving support from their family or from the medical personnel involved in their case—or who believed that the support they received was provided only out of a sense of duty—tended not to comply with restrictions on potassium and phosphorous.

The study also found that older patients followed health restrictions better than younger patients did. The authors suggest that this may be because older individuals tend to follow more routine and restricted life-styles than younger people do. This may make it easier for older patients to follow dietary restrictions as well.

Another possibility is that older people have a greater awareness of their own mortality and are more willing to take appropriate health precautions.

In addition, women were found to follow potassium restrictions more closely than men did. The researchers cannot account for this, although females in the study tended to believe that they were receiving more support from those around them than male patients did.

Another study, which appeared in the *International Journal of Aging and Human Development* (November-December 1990), also looked at older patients, this time examining the relationship between an individual's attitude toward life and his or her approach to dialysis. The researchers studied 315 patients who were over age 60 and who, on average, had been undergoing dialysis for almost five years. The report found that those individuals who had a generally positive outlook also tended to have a better view of their health and of dialysis treatment.

Therefore, the authors suggest that it is important to address the state of mind of elderly dialysis patients, perhaps with the help of counseling, physical or occupational therapy, and support from their peers.

A book entitled *The Many Faces of Suicide: Indirect Self-Destructive Behavior*, edited by Norman L. Farberow, provides further insight into the behavior of dialysis patients. One chapter, "The 'Uncooperative' Patient: Self-Destructive Behavior in Hemodialysis Patients," by Alan M. Goldstein, examines the idea that many patients who fail to follow a proper medical regimen may be trying to deny their health problems. In other words, the author suggests, the behavior of these individuals could be a way —albeit a potentially dangerous one—of coping with their illness.

"Patients on long-term hemo-dialysis encounter, at every moment, 'reminders' of the severity of their condition and the tenuous hold they maintain on life," Goldstein writes.

He believes that such actions can be viewed as a mechanism patients use to try to prove to themselves that they are not as ill as they fear.

According to Goldstein, studies indicate that those dialysis patients who successfully follow their treatment regimen tend to be self-reliant people who have found productive ways of dealing with their illness. He suggests that uncooperative patients can be helped by providing them with similar, healthy coping mechanisms.

The most frequent complication in acute renal failure is infection—which can cause death if uncontrolled.

CHRONIC RENAL FAILURE

Chronic renal failure evolves over an extended period, from as little as 2 to 3 months to as long as 30 to 40 years. It can result from a variety of conditions, including chronic glomerulonephritis, pyelonephritis, kidney injuries, atherosclerosis, and obstructive kidney stones.

During the early stages of chronic renal failure, the body is able to adjust to the slow loss of kidney function, and the patient usually exhibits no symptoms. By the time symptoms become obvious, 75% or more of all functional nephrons have been destroyed. At this point, glomerular filtration is at a fraction of its normal level and toxic wastes are beginning to accumulate in the bloodstream. Paradoxically, this stage is marked by increased urination (*polyuria*), because water and sodium are not being properly reabsorbed from the damaged kidneys. Moreover, as an individual loses water in this manner, he or she drinks more to make up the deficit, a cycle resulting in even higher urine production.

There is also increased nighttime urination (*nocturia*) at this stage. Under normal circumstances, much of the reabsorption of fluid from the renal tubules back into the bloodstream occurs at night—which explains the low amount of urine that is formed while an individual is asleep. When chronic renal failure occurs, this pattern is disrupted, accounting for the increase in urination at that time.

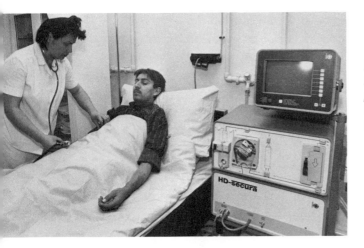

Patients in renal failure require dialysis to prevent harmful toxins from accumulating in the bloodstream.

The next stage of renal failure is called either *end-stage failure*, *uremic syndrome*, or uremia. At this point, 90% of the nephrons have been destroyed, and the glomerular filtration rate is at only 10% of normal functioning. Toxic metabolic waste products accumulate in the bloodstream, and unless a patient is placed on dialysis, a life-threatening condition develops.

Uremic Syndrome

When the kidneys fail to function, a series of reactions affect all systems of the body. Because so many nephrons are not functioning, metabolic wastes accumulate in the bloodstream. Failure to eliminate hydrogen ions causes the plasma to become acidic.

Another problem, as previously mentioned, is the buildup of potassium in the bloodstream—and the possible heart problems that may result. Normally, about 80% of potassium intake is eliminated through the urine.

During the later stages of renal failure, it is also common for blood sodium levels to increase as the kidneys lose the capacity to excrete electrolytes. The retained sodium attracts water, resulting in edema and elevated blood pressure and endangering the heart and the respiratory system.

Anemia, or a decrease in red blood cells, is a typical symptom. Normally *erythropoietin*, a substance released by healthy kidneys, stimulates red blood cell production. During renal failure the kidneys do not produce erythropoietin; hence, the red blood cell count goes down. Additionally, the changing chemistry in the plasma causes the existing red blood cells to rupture—resulting in a significant decrease in the life span of the red blood cell. As a result, the anemic patient often is pale and weak.

Uremia is also characterized by an increase in uric acid levels in the plasma because less uric acid is being eliminated from the body. When these levels rise, uric acid crystals may be deposited in joints and soft tissues, leading to gout.

Skin color often changes during this stage, because of an accumulation of the urinary *pigment* (color-producing substance) called *urochrome* in the bloodstream. The result is a waxy yellowish skin tone in whites, a yellowish-brown color in brown-skinned people, and an ashen-gray hue in blacks. In cases where urea concentration in the blood is extremely high there might even be a deposit of fine white urea crystals on the skin surface—referred to as *uremic frost*. Multiple bruises might also appear from the bleeding of fragile capillaries.

Because of a decrease in the glomerular filtration rate, urea and creatinine levels in the bloodstream increase. The rise of these and other toxins in the blood is believed to be responsible for a number of problems that occur in cases of uremia, including poor appetite, nausea, and vomiting. As a result, the patient loses weight, and there is frequently a urinelike smell on the breath. Open sores that bleed severely may form in the stomach and intestines. The resulting blood loss can lower blood pressure, further depressing the glomerular filtration rate.

Uremia is also associated with changes in the skeleton. Vitamin D, essential to the absorption of calcium from the gastrointestinal tract into the bloodstream, is modified for this purpose with the help of the kidneys. In the absence of normal kidney function, calcium concentration in the blood decreases, and sufficient amounts cannot be deposited in the bones. Simultaneously, deficient levels of blood calcium trigger the release of parathyroid hormone, which causes the release of calcium from bone tissue. The loss of calcium weakens the skeleton and paves the way for the deposition of calcium in soft tissue throughout the body. Calcification is a particular danger if it occurs in the heart, kidneys, or lungs.

In later stages of uremia, the nervous system is affected. Early symptoms of nerve damage include poor concentration, fatigue, and weakness. Restlessness and insomnia may also result. Sometimes the conduction of impulses through the nerves will slow down. Burning pain, numbness, and tingling of the toes and feet may progress up the leg.

Eventually, uremia can lead to convulsions and coma. Blood pressure falls progressively and then rapidly in the last few hours before death.

CHAPTER 7

DIALYSIS AND TRANSPLANT

During the 1940s, Dutch physician Willem Kolff developed a primitive but promising hemodialysis machine.

In the past, patients with irreversible renal failure inevitably died. But today, two lifesaving options are available to persons suffering from uremia: dialysis and transplant.

DIALYSIS

As previously discussed, dialysis involves cleansing the blood of metabolic wastes through the use of an apparatus that allows the exchange of particles between plasma and a specially balanced fluid called the dialysate.

During the 1940s, Dutch physician Willem Kolff developed an apparatus that could filter toxins and wastes from the bloodstream. Although primitive at first, the kidney machine provided a basis for further study and improvement. In 1947, Kolff donated the blueprints for his kidney machine to Peter Bent Brigham Hospital in Boston. Later, Kolff immigrated to the United States and became instrumental in refining the nature and mechanism of dialysis.

Dialysis depends upon passive transport, again involving the natural tendency of substances to move from an area of greater concentration to an area of lesser concentration until *equilibrium* (the equality of concentrations in both areas) is reached.

In dialysis, two fluids are also separated by a selectively permeable membrane: One fluid is blood, and the other is an artificially created dialysate solution that is in balance with the needs of the body. Toxins or wastes in the plasma move across the membrane to be flushed from the system, carrying with them excess salts or other undesirable particles. Only substances too large to pass through the pores of the membrane—such as protein molecules or red blood cells—will remain in the blood rather than be eliminated.

Peter Bent Brigham Hospital in Boston, where Willem Kolff donated the blueprints for his kidney machine. Dr. Kolff later immigrated to the United States and was instrumental in refining his invention.

Although the basic principles of dialysis are very simple, the mechanics of connecting a patient to a machine have proved problematic. There are two basic ways for dialysis to occur. One is to bring the blood through a machine that contains a membrane and dialysate fluid. This method is called *hemodialysis*. The alternative involves putting the dialysate into the abdominal cavity and using the body's own *peritoneal membrane* (the membrane that lines the abdominal cavity and covers the organs) to separate the blood from the dialysate. This process is called *peritoneal dialysis*.

Hemodialysis

The major difficulty in hemodialysis arose from the need to attach the patient to the machine with needles: one inserted into an artery, from which blood enters the machine, and one inserted into a vein, through which blood returns to the body. Gradually, as needles are repeatedly inserted into veins and arteries for continuing dialysis treatments, the blood vessels may be damaged.

Two techniques are used to avoid this problem. The first is the creation of an artificial connection of silicone rubber tubing between an artery and a vein. This tubing, called a *shunt*, is left outside the body and can be readily connected to a machine. Although the shunt can be used for months or years, its exposure to the air carries with it the danger of infection.

An alternative method, and the one normally used today, is the direct surgical attachment of an artery to a vein. Referred to as a *fistula*, this attachment also creates a viable connection to the kidney machine, while considerably reducing the danger of infection.

Another drawback to hemodialysis is the possibility of blood clotting in the tubes of the machine. This problem can usually be averted by administering heparin, an *anticoagulant* (anticlotting) drug.

Whereas dialysis was once used to prolong life during an acute, short-term episode of renal failure, it is now used for long periods of time when necessary. In 1990, more than 129,000 people in the United States were on hemo- or peritoneal dialysis, according to the U.S. Health Care financing Administration.

Kidney Donations:
Ethical Concerns

Do kidney patients—regardless of race or economic circumstances—share equally in the distribution of precious donor organs? The answer, it appears, is no. Studies and news reports indicate that, in some cases, economic and social factors both play a role in the allocation of kidneys for transplant.

DONOR ORGANS FOR SALE

A shortage of available transplant organs has led to the creation of a for-profit market for body parts. An example of this came to light several years ago, in the case of a British man who received a kidney transplant at a London hospital. After his death, it was discovered that the organ had literally been sold to the patient by a man from Turkey, who received $3,300 for the kidney, according to an article in the *New York Times* (August 1, 1989). As a result of this transaction, the British government placed a ban on the sale of transplant organs. Many other nations have similar laws or policies, but the issue remains a matter of international concern.

For example, according to an article in the medical journal *The Lancet* (June 22, 1991), it has been estimated that in India more than 2,000 kidneys annually have been taken from live donors and sold. The donors have been impoverished people seeking a handsome fee.

TRANSPLANTS AMONG MINORITY AND LOW-INCOME PATIENTS

Controversy also surrounds the apparent inequity of transplant operations in the United States among black and low-income kidney patients. A report in the *New England Journal of Medicine* (January 31, 1991) indicates that black patients are less likely to receive kidney transplants than white patients in need of such surgery. The study cites figures from the U.S. Health Care Financing Administration indicating that in 1985, 28% of patients suffering from a shutdown of kidney function were black; however, blacks represented only 21% of those receiving a kidney transplant.

Such data has proved particularly troubling because blacks are four times more likely to suffer kidney failure than whites are. (As previously discussed, high blood pressure can cause serious kidney damage, although this does not appear to be the only cause of the higher rate of renal failure among blacks.) Moreover, a 1990 report from the U.S. Department of Health and Human Services found that blacks wait an average of 13.9 months for a kidney transplant, compared to 7.6 months on average for white patients.

The reasons behind these disparities remain uncertain, although several factors may contribute. The American Medical Association Council on Ethics and Judicial Affairs has suggested that the medical community may practice some sort "subconscious bias" when choosing transplant candidates.

Another factor behind the shortage of kidneys for minorities appears to be biological. Scientists have encountered difficulty in finding a tissue match between a black patient and a white donor's kidney. In order for a transplant to be successful— that is, to prevent the body from rejecting the new organ—the donor and recipient must share certain cell molecules called *antigens*. Because some antigens found commonly in whites occur much less frequently in blacks, transplant success may be affected.

The problem has been made worse by the relatively small number of blacks who donate organs after death. In 1990, for example, only 9% of deceased kidney donors were black, compared to 83% who were white, according to the United Network for Organ Sharing. (Other minorities accounted for the rest of the donors.) The 1991 *New England Journal of Medicine* article suggests that minorities may not have been well informed about organ donation programs. Religious reservations concerning this practice and a distrust of the medical community may each play a part as well.

Money may be another factor in the lack of transplants among blacks. *Medicare*—a federally funded health program—pays a large part of transplant costs for patients. Yet hospitals may be reluctant to perform the surgery on economically disadvantaged people who cannot pay the remaining costs.

Clearly, a number of social and economic issues must be settled before every patient who needs a kidney transplant has equal access to donor organs.

In this 1986 photo, Utah senator Jake Garn leaves Georgetown University Hospital with his daughter Susan after having donated a kidney to her a week earlier. The young woman's own kidneys had failed as a result of damage from diabetes.

When doctors first began using dialysis for chronic renal failure, the time demands on patients were tremendous. Usually a patient would have to be hospitalized, hooked up to a machine, and administered dialysis for 10 to 12 hours at a time. Moreover, this procedure had to be repeated two to three times a week, so treatment was primarily limited to those people who lived near a medical center where dialysis was available. Lives were disrupted, vacations were out of the question, and patients were literally prisoners of their illnesses.

Now, home peritoneal dialysis and hemodialysis have become realistic options. Modern technology has produced smaller, more efficient machines, prepackaged dialysate solutions, and easy-to-use connectors. To be approved for home treatment, patients have to be evaluated on several different fronts. They must be strongly motivated, willing and able to pay attention to detail, and have a friend or relative who can help with the procedure. Children are often good candidates for home dialysis and can thus be freed from the restrictions of hospital-based treatments. The invention of a miniature artificial kidney machine has also been liberating, allowing patients in renal failure to get away on vacation for short periods of two to three weeks at a time.

Despite the advances made in hemodialysis, the procedure still poses problems. Blood vessel sites available for hookup to a machine are limited, and some people feel overwhelmed by the machine and their dependence on it. In addition, hemodialysis sometimes leaves patients feeling washed-out and weak.

Peritoneal Dialysis

For those seeking an alternative to hemodialysis, peritoneal dialysis may be an option. By this method, fluid is run into the abdomen through a rubber tube. Some time is allotted for the exchange of particles between body fluids and the dialysate liquid. Then the abdominal area is flushed out, and fresh dialysate is introduced.

César Milstein, who, with Georges Köhler, shared a Nobel Prize in 1984 for the discovery of OKT3, an advanced immunosuppressant.

In intermittent peritoneal dialysis, the procedure is performed 3 to 4 times a week, with dialysis lasting between 10 to 14 hours. In continuous peritoneal dialysis, fluid is run into the abdomen, left for several hours, and replaced four or more times a day. Between fluid exchanges, the patient is not hooked up to a machine and is free to participate in normal activities. One drawback to the peritoneal method, however, is the danger of infection. Because fluid must be changed frequently, precautions must be taken to prevent the entry of bacteria into the abdominal cavity. Despite meticulous care, most patients on continuous peritoneal dialysis develop *peritonitis* (an inflammation of the peritoneal membrane) at least once a year. A physician's decision of whether to use hemodialysis or peritoneal dialysis depends upon the individual patient.

Treatment Issues

As dialysis became a treatment of choice for individuals in renal failure, moral and ethical dilemmas began to surface. Originally, the demand for dialysis was great, but the supply limited. Someone or some group had to pass judgment and decide who was to be favored with treatment. Criteria were varied. Some thought that young people should be given priority. Others believed that the value of a person to the community should enter into the equation. Ultimately the question became extremely complicated. Who could say that a young mother with three children was less valuable than a single brilliant research scientist at the peak of his or her career?

Fortunately, the availability of hemodialysis centers has increased over time, and the supply now approximates the demand. But the question of expense is still an issue. The cost of dialysis is approximately $25,000 per year. Few people can afford such an outlay, and insurance companies have been reluctant to cover such a costly procedure. To help ensure that kidney patients receive proper care, in 1972 the federal government made dialysis patients eligible for *Medicare* benefits. (Medicare is the federal health insurance program for the elderly and severely disabled.)

Despite a concerted effort by such organizations as the National Kidney Foundation, the percentage of transplant organs available from the potential pool of donors remains low.

RENAL TRANSPLANT

Although dialysis can prolong life for people in renal failure, the ultimate goal is to free patients from a restrictive dependence upon machines, tubes, and needles. The ideal situation, if damage to both kidneys is irreversible, is to transplant a healthy kidney successfully into a patient and return him or her to a full range of unrestricted activities.

Over the years, with the help of advances such as the immuno-suppressant cyclosporine, kidney transplant successes have increased markedly. In the forefront of more recent advances is the drug OKT3, which consists of *monoclonal antibodies*. These laboratory-produced antibodies seem to be able to specifically inactivate the body's anti-transplant immune response, leaving the rest of the immune system intact. They are believed to do this by affecting certain immune cells and rendering them unable to function in the rejection of the transplant.

With advanced technology providing the means to mediate immuno-suppression, the problem of inadequate organ supply still remains to be solved. In spite of efforts by organizations such as the National Kidney Foundation to increase public support, the United Network for Organ Sharing estimates that only 33% to 40% of the potential pool of deceased organ donors (for all organs) is being tapped.

A 1967 law allows people to give permission for their organs to be donated after their death by signing a *uniform donor card*. If no donor card exists, health care professionals will often approach the bereft family of a brain-dead accident victim for permission to use organs for transplant. Not surprisingly, seeking such permission can be a very difficult task at a tragic time. Many families find it difficult to accept that their loved one is brain-dead. They often feel repelled by the thought of removing body parts—albeit for a good cause.

The shortage of organs has led to ethical questions and dilemmas. What about the case of Aaron Rowe, who, unemployed for three months, offered to sell a kidney or eye for $10,000? What about Jamie Fiske, an 11-month-old child who needed a new liver? Her father, a

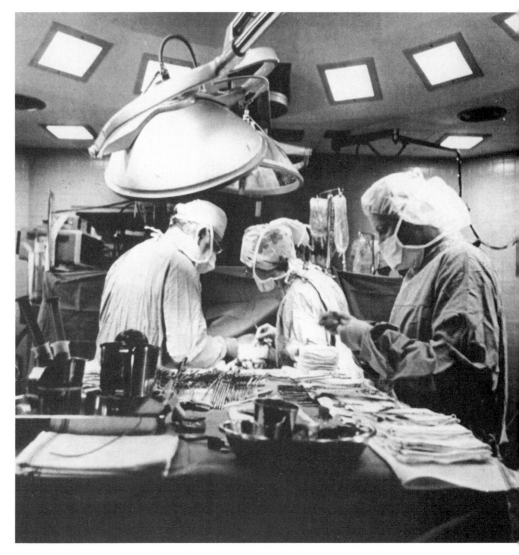

In 1982, surgeons at the University of Minnesota Hospital performed a liver transplant on 11-month-old Jamie Fiske. Her case and others have brought to light various ethical concerns regarding the limited supply of donor organs.

hospital administrator, had the means and knowledge to mount a national publicity campaign that resulted in his obtaining an organ for his daughter. Should people be allowed to sell their organs to the highest bidder? Should a patient of wealth and means be allowed to take priority over an equally needy but socioeconomically disadvantaged patient on a waiting list for months or years?

Today, an increasing number of successful transplants are being performed. Moreover, if a transplant fails, patients may return for second or third grafts without diminishing their chances for success. Forty years after the first kidney transplant was attempted, monumental strides offer hope for patients in end-stage renal failure.

APPENDIX

APPENDIX:
FOR MORE INFORMATION

The following is a list of organizations that can provide further information about kidney disorders, transplants, and organ donation.

GENERAL INFORMATION

Channing L. Bete, Inc.
45 Federal Street
Greenfield, MA 01301

Eli Lilly and Company
Public Relations Services
P.O. Box 618
Indianapolis, IN 46206
(317) 636-2211

The National Association of Patients on
    Hemodialysis and Transplantation
505 Northern Blvd.
Great Neck, NY 11021
(516) 482-2720

National Kidney Foundation
2 Park Avenue
New York, NY 10016
(212) 889-2210

National Kidney Foundation of New
    York/New Jersey, Inc.
1250 Broadway, Suite 2001
New York, NY 10001
(212) 629-9770

(516) 222-1883
(201) 342-7894

National Kidney Foundation of
    Southern California
5777 Century Blvd., Suite 395
Los Angeles, CA 90045
(213) 641-8152

Parke Davis and Company
Patient Education
201 Tabor Road
Morris Plains, NJ 07950
(201) 540-2000

ORGAN DONATION

LifeBanc
1909 East 101 Street
Cleveland, OH 44106
(216) 791-5433

Pittsburgh Transplant Foundation
5743 Center Avenue
Pittsburgh, PA 15206
(412) 336-6777

FURTHER READING

American Medical Association Staff. *The American Medical Association Family Medical Guide.* New York: Random House, 1987.

Boulton-Jones, M. *Acute and Chronic Renal Failure.* Norwell, MA: Kluwer Academic, 1982.

Cameron, Stewart. *Kidney Disease: The Facts.* New York: Oxford University Press, 1986.

Cummings, Nancy B., and Saulo Klahr, eds. *Chronic Renal Disease: Causes, Complications, and Treatment.* New York: Plenum, 1985.

Farberow, Norman L., ed. *The Many Faces of Suicide: Indirect Self-Destructive Behavior.* New York: McGraw-Hill Book Company, 1980.

Gabriel, R. *A Patient's Guide to Dialysis and Transplantation.* Norwell, MA: Kluwer Academic, 1987.

Miller, Martha J. *Pathophysiology: Principles of Disease.* Philadelphia: Saunders, 1983.

Oberley, Edith T., and Neal R. Glass. *Understanding Kidney Transplantation.* Springfield, IL: Thomas, 1987.

Phillips, Robert H. *Coping with Kidney Failure: A Guide to Living with Kidney Failure for You and Your Family.* Garden City Park, NY: Avery, 1987.

Price, Sylvia, and Lorraine Wilson. *Pathophysiology: Clinical Concepts of Disease Processes.* New York: McGraw-Hill, 1978.

Rotellar, Carlos. *Acute Renal Insufficiency Made Ridiculously Simple.* North Miami Beach: Medmaster, N. d.

Smith, William A. *Gout and the Gouty.* San Antonio: Naylor, 1970.

Spencer, Karen. *A Patient's Guide to Understanding Kidney Disease.* Sacramento: Anderson, 1987.

Williams, D. Gwynn. *Renal Disease: An Illustrated Guide.* Norwell, MA: Kluwer Academic, 1982.

GLOSSARY

acute postinfectious glomerulonephritis an inflammation of the glomerulus often resulting from a recent streptococcal infection of the throat or skin or other serious bacterial and viral infection; symptoms include decreased urine output, darkening of the urine, fluid retention, shortness of breath, and high blood pressure

aldosterone a hormone secreted by the adrenal cortex that regulates the amount of water, sodium, chloride, and potassium in the bloodstream

antidiuretic hormone (ADH) vasopressin; a hormone that increases blood pressure and has a diuretic effect

arterioles small, branching arteries that transport blood to the capillaries

arteriosclerosis the thickening of the walls of the arterioles, causing them to lose their elasticity

Bowman's capsule a membranous cup that surrounds the glomerulus and acts as a filter in the formation of urine

calculi kidney stones

chronic glomerulonephritis an inflammation of the glomerulus that may develop from a variety of diseases, including a case of acute glomerulonephritis that fails to disappear; symptoms include loss of appetite, nausea and vomiting, extreme fatigue, difficulty sleeping, itching and dry skin, and muscle cramps occurring at night

collecting duct a small tubule that collects urine from several nephrons and discharges it into the pelvis (the basin-shaped cavity) of the kidney

cystitis a bladder infection, the symptoms of which include frequent and painful urination and blood in the urine

cystoscopy the insertion of an instrument called a cystoscope through the urethra to examine the bladder and ureters

dialysis a method of removing waste, salt, and extra water from the body when the kidneys are no longer able to function

distal convoluted tubule (DCT) a tubule that lies between the loop of Henle and the collecting duct

diuretic a substance that increases the flow of urine

edema dropsy; an accumulation of fluid in the body's tissues

erythropoietin a hormone released by the kidneys that regulates red blood cell production; when the kidneys fail, erythropoietin is not formed, resulting in anemia (a decrease in red blood cells)

extracorporeal shock wave lithotripsy a medical procedure using shock waves generated outside the body to crush kidney stones into tiny particles that can be passed out of the body in urine

filtration the process by which the kidneys produce urine

glomerulus an intertwined mass of capillaries contained in the Bowman's capsule; the filtering part of the kidneys

gout an acute form of arthritis caused by an overproduction of uric acid in the blood or by the kidney's inability to properly remove uric acid from the body

hemodialysis a type of dialysis in which the blood is cleaned outside the body; an artificial kidney is hooked up to an artery and a vein, blood enters the machine from the artery, is cleaned with a solution called dialysate, and returns to the body through the vein

homeostasis the maintenance of stable internal physiological conditions

hydronephrosis the enlargement of the kidney as a result of an accumulation of urine in the renal pelvis and accompanied by atrophy of the kidney structure and the formation of a cyst

loop of Henle a U-shaped loop that plays a role in water reabsorption and is part of the nephron

nephritis an acute or chronic inflammation of the kidneys that may be caused by a variety of factors, including bacteria, toxic drugs, and alcohol

nephron renal tubule; the functional unit of the kidney; there are approximately 1 million nephrons in each kidney

nocturia excessive urination during the night

papillae renal papillae; structures in the kidneys that drain urine into the renal pelvis

perineal lithotomy the removal of kidney stones through an incision made in the groin

peritoneal dialysis a type of dialysis in which the blood is cleaned inside the body; dialysate enters the abdominal (peritoneal) space through a plastic tube that has been surgically placed into the lower abdomen, and wastes from the bloodstream pass through the peritoneal membrane lining the abdominal cavity into the cleansing fluid; after the filtration is complete, the waste-containing fluid leaves the body through the tube

polycystic kidney disease (PKD) a hereditary disease characterized by the formation of cysts in the kidneys and that may result in kidney failure; symptoms include enlargement of both kidneys, back pain, blood in the urine, kidney stones, recurring bladder or kidney infections, and high blood pressure

polyuria excessive urination

prostate gland a gland, found only in males, that surrounds the neck of the bladder and the urethra; the enlargement of the prostate may cause it to squeeze on the urethra, thereby impeding the flow of urine

proximal convoluted tubule (PCT) a small tube leading from the Bowman's capsule to the loop of Henle through which fluid absorbed from the bloodstream travels; while in the PCT, water, sodium, chloride, sugar, calcium, proteins, and amino acids are absorbed back into the bloodstream, and the remaining fluid is released as urine

pyelonephritis a kidney infection usually caused by bacteria entering the kidney through the urethra; symptoms include a frequent need to urinate, severe pain in the lower back, headache, fever, and chills

renal pertaining to the kidneys

sphincter muscle a muscle around the opening of the urethra that controls urination

supra-pubic lithotomy the removal of kidney stones through an incision made above the abdomen

urea an odorless, colorless substance produced by proteins in the body that is the main component in mammalian urine

uremic syndrome end-stage renal failure; uremia; permanent, irreversible damage to both kidneys requiring dialysis or a kidney transplant

ureter a tube that carries urine from the kidney to the bladder

urethra a canal that leads from the bladder to the outside of the body for the discharge of urine

uric acid an odorless and tasteless white acid found in small quantities in mammalian urine; an excess amount of uric acid can result in gout

urinary bladder a muscular, membranous sac that temporarily stores urine prior to urination

urinary tract the organs and vessels involved in the production and elimination of urine

urine excess water and waste removed from the bloodstream by the kidneys, stored in the bladder, and discharged through the urethra

INDEX

PICTURE CREDITS

Martha J. Miller has a degree in Human Anatomy and Physiology from Mt. Holyoke College and an MAT degree in Biology from Yale University. For 13 years she taught anatomy and physiology to health career students and designed and taught courses in fluids and electrolytes, pathology, and pathophysiology. She is the author of *Pathophysiology: Principles of Disease*, which was published by the W.B. Saunders Company in 1983 and currently resides in California, where she does freelance writing.

Dale C. Garell, M.D., is medical director of California Children Services, Department of Health Services, County of Los Angeles. He is also associate dean for curriculum at the University of Southern California School of Medicine and clinical professor in the Department of Pediatrics & Family Medicine at the University of Southern California School of Medicine. From 1963 to 1974, he was medical director of the Division of Adolescent Medicine at Children's Hospital in Los Angeles. Dr. Garell has served as president of the Society for Adolescent Medicine, chairman of the youth committee of the American Academy of Pediatrics, and as a forum member of the White House Conference on Children (1970) and White House Conference on Youth (1971). He has also been a member of the editorial board of the *American Journal of Diseases of Children.*

C. Everett Koop, M.D., Sc.D., is former Surgeon General, deputy assistant secretary for health, and director of the Office of International Health of the U.S. Public Health Service. A pediatric surgeon with an international reputation, he was previously surgeon-in-chief of Children's Hospital of Philadelphia and professor of pediatric surgery and pediatrics at the University of Pennsylvania. Dr. Koop is the author of more than 175 articles and books on the practice of medicine. He has served as surgery editor of the *Journal of Clinical Pediatrics* and editor-in-chief of the *Journal of Pediatric Surgery.* Dr. Koop has received nine honorary degrees and numerous other awards, including the Denis Brown Gold Medal of the British Association of Paediatric Surgeons, the William E. Ladd Gold Medal of the American Academy of Pediatrics, and the Copernicus Medal of the Surgical Society of Poland. He is a chevalier of the French Legion of Honor and a member of the Royal College of Surgeons, London.